*Concealed Weapon Carry: Mississippi Laws*

For more information please contact:
Springmorningpublishing@info.com

Cover photo and interior photos part of author's personal, or purchased collection unless otherwise noted.

Printed in the United States of America

*Concealed Weapon Carry: Mississippi Laws*

Rick Ward

1. How-to - 2. Reference - 3. Constitutional Rights - 4. Civil Rights - 5. Law - 6. Crime - 7. Weapons - 8. Guns - 9. Permits - 10. Training - 11. Mississippi

Library of Congress Control Number: 2012904580

ISBN-10: 0982809956

ISBN-13: 978-0-9828099-5-2

SPRING
MORNING

PUBLISHING

http://www.sprngmorningpublishing.com

# FORWARD

House Bill 506, a measure adopted by the legislature and signed into law by Governor Haley Barbour in 2011, was aimed at extending the rights and obligations available under Mississippi's concealed carry laws to officers of the court, specifically, our prosecutors and public defenders. As the bill moved through the legislative process, it was amended to include all Mississippians who voluntarily complete a nationally certified course in the safe handling and use of firearms.

As the author of the bill, I was encouraged by the work of numerous colleagues in the legislature who labored to create a law that would allow law abiding Mississippians to enjoy the same rights and protections already established in many of our sister states. Our hope continues to be that this law will serve to make Mississippi families safer.

I am pleased that my friend, Rick Ward, has taken time to help make this law and all laws pertaining to the safe handling of firearms more understandable for the general public. This is an important public service and valuable tool for those of us deeply concerned with firearm safety.

This book has been a labor of love for Rick and with his extensive law enforcement background, I can think of no one better qualified to introduce our new law to the citizens of Mississippi. It is my hope that Rick's work will be widely read and taken to heart.

*Brandon Jones*
Mississippi House of Representatives 2007-2012

# Concealed Weapon Carry:

# Mississippi Laws

by

Rick Ward

# Table of Contents

# PREFACE

I want to preface what you read in this book by saying that under no circumstances am I representing myself as a lawyer, or offering you any legal advice whatsoever.

I will say that I am familiar with the law, having worked as a law enforcement officer in Mississippi in various positions for over fourteen years. I have been a uniformed police officer, state narcotics officer, chief criminal investigator, attorney general public integrity investigator, medicaid fraud investigator, gaming commission division director, and federal employment compensation act fraud investigator.

I also served twenty years in the navy, sixteen of which were in law enforcement, physical security, antiterrorism and force protection. I have carried weapons into, and through many states, on airplanes and in foreign countries.

I have an adept ability to read, understand and interpret the laws of this state, and I will do my best to do so throughout this book, without offering you any advice or representing myself as an attorney. However, I can read and make informed decisions on my own.

I may at times tell you, based on my interpretation of the law, what I would do in given circumstances, but that in no way is a recommendation for you to follow my lead.

I am providing copies of various laws and will discuss them, as well as shooting scenarios, that have made the news in recent years and pertain to this subject.

If you are involved in a shooting, you can just about be guaranteed a law suit, if not criminal charges, depending on the judgment you used in the situation. I strongly encourage you to practice your drawing and shooting techniques, and consult an attorney before it happens, just to be on the safe side. You must understand the law <u>before</u> that happens.

# ACKNOWLEDGMENT

I want to thank God for continuing my life on September 11, 1976. While serving as a uniformed police officer at Moss Point, MS, I was in the dispatch office along with a few other officers and the dispatcher.

A well-known citizen who was also a county road patrolman and part-time deputy sheriff, walked into the police station without a shirt on. We could only see him from about waist up through the ticket paying window.

As he rounded the corner and approached the entry door to dispatch, he raised a .357 Magnum, Colt Trooper blue steel revolver, pointing it in the direction of the dispatcher. The gun was right in front of my chest though pointing at the dispatcher, as he ordered her to call in all units.

He was angry about me arresting his part-time thug employer who ran a dump truck business under questionable contracts issued by his brother.... the Mayor. Yes this drunken assailant was the Mayor's brother and the President of the Board of Supervisor's County Road Patrolman. The anger resulted from a newspaper story where I had arrested his boss and other thugs the night before. They were required to spend at least six hours in jail before being released. However since he was a part-time employee of the arrested dump truck owners, he was called and told to go get his brother and get them out of jail, not six hours later, but right then. He had done so the night before. They were indeed released within the hour as revealed by the newspaper reporter that reviewed the jail docket every morning.

The Mayor freaked. His drunk brother went crazy, blaming us for the article. He wanted the dispatcher to call all units in so they could see what was about to happen, something "shocking" to go to the newspaper about.

Barry Jones, an alert detective listening to his walkie-talkie down the hall heard the call and sneaked up behind the drunk, whose back was exposed to the hallway. Barry shoved his 45 Colt into the right side of the drunk's head, demanding he drop the weapon. However, the drunk rotated the gun to his left, at me, and straight in front of my face. I grabbed it with my left hand under the barrel and tried to get my right hand in front of the cocked hammer. He jerked downward on the weapon, and pulled the trigger before I could get my right hand in place. It shot me through the web of my left hand, with the muzzle blast burning my face, eyebrows and left sideburns.

I was treated at the hospital for a gunshot wound received in the line of duty. He received severe injuries from other officers while resisting arrest afterwards. His boss, the dump truck owner, later went to federal prison. His other boss, the President of the Board of Supervisors was later indicted and removed from office on other issues by the Attorney General. His brother, the Mayor only got 366 votes (out of about twenty thousand) for re-election a few months later. The shooter became a convicted felon.

A .357 magnum super-velocity jacketed hollow-point bullet missed my left eye socket by about two inches. But I lived to tell about it, and spent thirteen more years in civilian law enforcement, as well as sixteen in military law enforcement before retiring.

# INTRODUCTION

I recently started taking an Enhanced Carry Course myself. I don't like taking my weapon off and putting it back on depending on what building I go in. The new law enables one to carry a weapon in just about any building except police stations, courtrooms in session and places of nuisance. However, the state law does not apply to federal facilities. I have no need to carry one in either of those places anyway, so the law suits me just fine.

I believe the Mississippi Highway Patrol has done a good job implementing a program that may have just landed in their laps. However, after reviewing some of the materials instructors were authorized to use, and seeing that there was information lacking, I decided to write my own manual and seek my own instructor certification. I dropped out of the Enhanced Carry Class to pursue my own instructor certification even though that had been the furthest thing from my mind before that.

I believe instructors teaching Concealed Carry courses, should begin with the basics. We always say safety is first and it is. However, you need to know **what** a concealed weapon is before you even start to pick one up. Once you learn what a concealed weapon is, and what the law is, you may find that you don't need a permit at all.

I believe you need to know those basics first. Then you should begin to familiarize yourself with firearms and which one would be best for you. I think you need to know what concealment method is best for you and show up at your class with your gun and holster. You should receive further familiarization in class, along with safety and the law. Your instructor should be very familiar with the law and not blurt out so-called laws that don't exist that may cause him to lose credibility.

It is no big mystery, or miracle as to why those state/city pistol team members can shoot the center out of targets at fifty yards. You should learn a lesson from that and practice as much as you can, because those guys do nothing but shoot, all day long on your tax dollars. If you were paid to do that job as your primary responsibility and all your ammunition was paid for, you might well be as good as they are. They have done it for years!

Know that practice makes perfect in quick draw and accuracy. Both may save your life, but another skill you must learn is, when to shoot. Judgmental shooting and economical shooting methods will be touched on.

# CHAPTER ONE

## Meaning of Concealed Weapons

In order to understand those things we need to know about concealed weapons, we need to first dissect the term "Carrying Concealed Weapons." We will address licenses, permits, and the enhanced portion of the law at a later time. After reading this, you may find you don't need one.

1. Carrying – Mississippi statutes do not address what the term "carrying" means. That is not to say that case law or Attorney General Opinions don't. Common sense would most likely dictate as it relates to the concealed weapons laws, that it means to carry on your person, or have it within reach or lunging distance. Black's law dictionary (online version) says it means to bear, bear about, sustain, transport, remove, or convey.

2. Concealed – Mississippi statutes are vague when it comes to the term "concealed." It goes on to say "in whole or in part." Throughout my police career, police officers said weapons are always concealed because even lying in the open on a car seat in plain view, at least one half of it (the other side) cannot be seen. I don't subscribe to that mentality, and I doubt if most legitimate judges would either. I don't think the term "concealed carry" existed when "in whole or in part" was added to the statute and the legislature is yet to define what "concealed" is. By looking at other states' definitions which vary widely, one would almost think the definition is vague by design. But let's go back to common sense and conclude that "concealed" means "can't be seen." So if an officer looking for it can't see it openly, he would have to search for it by opening, lifting or moving something in order to see it.

3.   Weapon – The Mississippi Legislature has long recognized the rights of hunters and by statute has left long guns designed for hunting in a special category. Title 97, Chapter 37, Section 1 (97-37-1), paragraph (1) of the Mississippi Code defines those dangerous weapons that mere possession of, can result in charges of Carrying Concealed Weapons. Those weapons are: any bowie knife, dirk knife, butcher knife, switchblade knife, metallic knuckles, blackjack, slingshot, pistol, revolver, or any rifle with a barrel of less than sixteen (16) inches in length, or any shotgun with a barrel of less than eighteen (18) inches in length, machine gun or any fully automatic firearm or deadly weapon, or any muffler or silencer for any firearm, whether or not it is accompanied by a firearm.

a. Most of the edged weapons listed above vary in design but usually have a long fixed blade and a short handle. Here are a few examples:

Bowie Knife

Dirk Knife

Butcher Knife

b. A switchblade differs in that it is usually spring-loading with a retractable, or folding blade, activated by the push of a button.

Switchblade Knife

c. Metallic knuckles are normally metallic (often brass) molds with four finger holes for the users' fingers, while having a bridge of metal across the top of the fingers used to cause bodily harm to an opponent when inflicting a blow. They are sometimes made of composite materials so as to avoid identification from metal detectors and they are lighter.

Metallic Knuckles

Metallic Knuckles made in the shape of California

d.  Blackjacks are described as any array of police baton, nightstick, or club type device, including tools used for truck drivers when checking air in their tires. They become a weapon if intended for the purpose of causing bodily harm or threatening bodily harm.

Police Baton

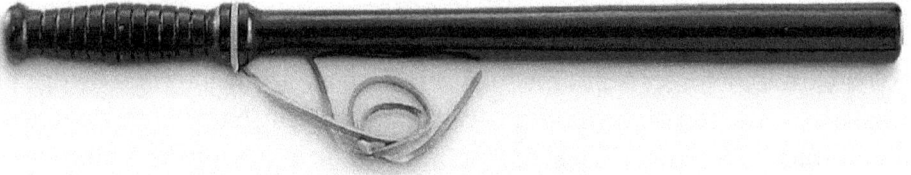

Short Version

Trucker's Tire Thumper

Trucker's Tire Buddies

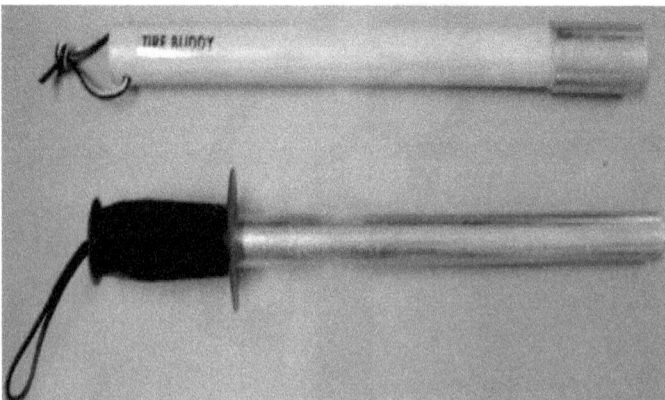

e. Slingshots are forked type wood, plastic or metal devices with elastic straps or tubes fitted to the top end of each fork, and joined by a pad in the middle of the strap that holds a projectile of some sort, be it rock, steel ball or similar device used as a projectile propelled by pulling the elastic mechanism back and releasing the projectile pad, hurling the projectile to its target.

Professional metal slingshot with wrist brace

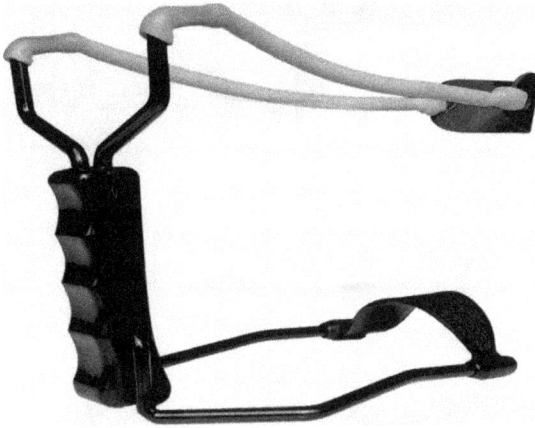

Home-made wooden slingshot

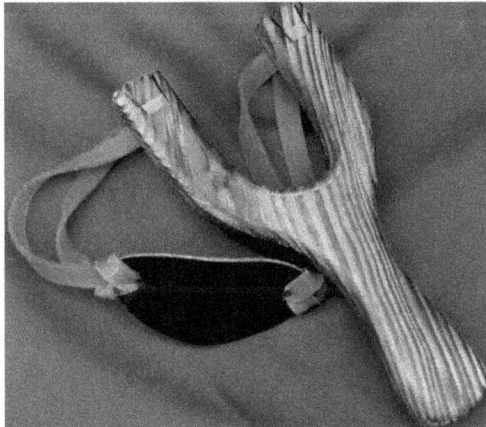

f.    Pistols are most often thought of today as semi-automatic handguns usually operated by gaseous discharges caused from the firing of the first round. Some have hammers, some are hammerless. A derringer that is neither semi-automatic, nor a revolver can fire one single bullet, two with one stacked on top of the other, or other configuration.

Hammerless .40 Caliber Glock

Beretta 9mm with hammer

Colt .25 Caliber semi-auto

Cobra 2 shot .38 Caliber Derringer

g. Revolvers are cylindrical operating handguns that usually carry six, but sometimes more or less rounds of ammunition with the revolver cylinder moving to the next shot from the pull of the trigger. Older types, or those designed under older standards may be "single action" in which the cylinder rotates as the hammer is pulled back. They can also be Derringers and can have hammers or be hammerless. This is only a few examples:

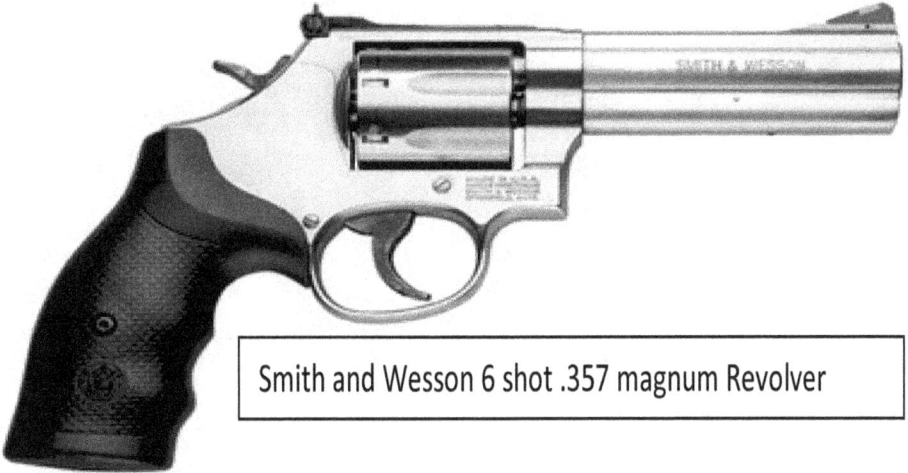

Smith and Wesson 6 shot .357 magnum Revolver

Taurus 5 shot .38 Caliber Revolver

Charter Arms 5 shot .22 Caliber Derringer

h. **Rifle with a barrel of less than sixteen (16) inches** in length. I am putting emphasis on this category with bold letters because it is so often misconstrued. Based on this definition, I do not believe a rifle (or shotgun) could be considered a concealed weapon (in Mississippi) if the barrel is 16 inches or longer, regardless of how it may be concealed. Unlike shotguns, rifles are rarely sawed off anyway because accuracy is decreased.

i. **Shotgun with a barrel of less than eighteen (18) inches** in length. While a shotgun can be a very dangerous weapon when sawed off because of its ability to spread multiple projectiles with one shot, **it is only considered a concealed weapon if the barrel is under 18 inches (no matter how concealed)**. Mississippi law does not address the overall length, but federal statutes do (barrels less than 18 inches, or overall length less than 26 inches is a violation of federal law).

This sawed off shotgun is legal in Mississippi (barrel is over 18 inches) and under federal law since the overall length is more than 26 inches. Based on Mississippi statutes, this weapon **cannot** be considered a concealed weapon, regardless of how it may be concealed. No permit is required.

# NOTE:

Be forewarned that many police officers have not read this statute word-for-word, or may work at a department where it has been customary practice to charge people with Carrying Concealed Weapons like this.

Most police departments are very busy and don't have time to charge people in gray areas. Maybe their judges have already faced these defenses from sharp lawyers that made a fool out of the officer, and arrests of this nature have stopped.

However, you may be exposed to a department who has too few tally marks on their arrests records submitted to the FBI. They may be a small department in a very civilized town, a campus police, or hospital police force with little crime and might jump at the opportunity to charge you.

If it was me, I would go to court by myself with a copy of this statute to present to the judge very respectfully in my defense if arrested for a concealed long gun. If found guilty anyway I would appeal, and hire a lawyer who knew the law better than me and get him, (or her) to represent me on appeal. I would not humor the officer up front by paying big bucks when he might have seen that issue as my punishment, knowing the charge was unlawful all along.

Most officers are honest and would not knowingly make a false charge, but there is always that one, or maybe he didn't know and your defense could make him a better, more knowledgeable officer. Whatever you do, and listed to this carefully, NEVER, EVER argue with an officer about to arrest you. I promise, you will lose. The courtroom is the place to argue your side. It may be hard to take, knowing you are right. However, you will get that chance to prove it. Arguing with an officer will only get you in more trouble and you probably won't get out of that, even if you were right in the first place.

## Defenses against charges of Carrying Concealed Weapons under Mississippi Law (97-37-1):

*1. It shall not be a violation of this section for any person over the age of eighteen (18) years to carry a firearm or deadly weapon:*

> *a. Within the confines of his own home*
> *b. Place of business*
> *c. Any real property associated with his home or business*
> *d. Within any motor vehicle*

*2. It shall not be a violation if the possessor is engaged in a legitimate weapon-related sports activity or is going to or returning from such activity as:*

> *a. Hunting*
> *b. Fishing*
> *c. Target shooting*
> *d. Or any other legal sports activity which normally involves the use of a firearm or other weapon.*

## Penalties:

(a)  By a fine of not less than One Hundred Dollars ($ 100.00) nor more than Five Hundred Dollars ($ 500.00), or by imprisonment in the county jail for not more than six (6) months, or both, in the discretion of the court, for the first conviction under this section.

(b)  By a fine of not less than One Hundred Dollars ($ 100.00) nor more than Five Hundred Dollars ($ 500.00), and imprisonment in the county jail for not less than thirty (30) days nor more than six (6) months, for the second conviction under this section.

(c)  By confinement in the custody of the Department of Corrections for not less than one (1) year nor more than five (5) years, for the third or subsequent conviction under this section.

(d)  By confinement in the custody of the Department of Corrections for not less than one (1) year nor more than ten (10) years for any person previously convicted of any felony who is convicted under this section.

Office of the Attorney General
State of Mississippi
Opinion No. 2011-00063

March 23, 2011

Re: Concealed Weapons in Vehicle

Gene Barton, Esquire
City of Okolona
Post Office Box 147
Okolona MS 38860
Dear Mr. Barton:

Attorney General Jim Hood has received your request for an opinion and has assigned it to me for research and reply. Your letter asks:

QUESTION

Specifically, the question has arisen as to whether or not under the statute as amended may a person carry, without a permit, a concealed weapon inside their vehicle which would include on the dashboard, on the seat, or in the glove compartment, or on their person if they are inside the vehicle and also may the person maintain in their own home a concealed weapon.

Our particular question has arisen concerning Concealed Weapons inside an automobile for example on the seat, under the seat, in the glove compartment or in the compartment between the seats.

RESPONSE

None of the factual situations described above would be a violation of the concealed weapons statute, assuming the defendant is 18 or older.

ANALYSIS

Section 97-37-1 of the Mississippi Code prohibits the carrying of a concealed weapon, but adds: It shall not be a violation of this section for any person over the age of eighteen (18) years to carry a firearm or deadly weapon concealed in whole or in part within the confines of his own home or his place of business, or any real property associated with his home or business or within any motor vehicle.

**Miss. Code Ann. Section 97-37-1 (2)**

Under this statute, having a pistol concealed under a blanket inside a van while driving around is not a crime. Knight v. State, 983 So.2d 348 (Miss. App. 2008) (ineffective assistance of counsel to allow defendant to plead guilty to concealed weapon charge under these facts). Likewise, it is our opinion that none of the instances cited in your letter would constitute a violation of 97-37-1 by a person over the age of 18.

Sincerely,

Jim Hood
Attorney General
By: Mike Lanford,
Special Assistant Attorney General

## Summary:

Based on Mississippi law, you are not required to have a permit or license to carry a concealed weapon in your home, place of business, or any real property associated with those structures.

You do not have to have a license, or permit to carry a concealed weapon in your car and unlike other states, Mississippi does not distinguish between loaded, unloaded, trunk, locked container, or anything else.

A shotgun or rifle can **never** be a concealed weapon regardless of how hidden unless it is sawed off below the legal limit.

You may carry any of those described weapons to, from, and during hunting and fishing expeditions, target shooting, or other events where those weapons would normally be allowed. However, you may have to prove those conditions if charged. Possession does not preclude an officer from charging you with the offense. The defense in that case is up to you. Remember though, the burden of proof is on the prosecution.

With regards to licenses or permits to carry concealed weapons, you may not need one. If you only carry a gun in your house, your car and your business and/or to sporting activities, you don't.

If you want to carry one concealed on your person in town, or on the streets or buildings other than your home or business, you do.

If you want to carry in public buildings or places not authorized with a regular concealed permit, you will need an enhanced carry endorsement. However there will still be some prohibited places.

Each of those will be explained in more detail. I will from time to time tell short "war stories" and highlight current events that deal with the subject of concealed weapons or use of force, so as not to make it so dry.

Speaking of current events, according to a recent article in USA Today, twelve states are considering legislation that would do away with their laws that require the issuance of weapon permits. March 12, 2012 online edition:

*States that have been or are considering bills in current legislative sessions include Colorado, Iowa, Georgia, Kentucky, Maine, New Hampshire, Ohio, Oklahoma, Rhode Island, South Carolina, South Dakota and Virgina, according to the NRA.*

*South Dakota could be the fifth state to join the ranks of permit-less carry states. Lawmakers last week passed a measure allowing anyone 18 and older with a valid state driver's license to carry a concealed weapon, as long as they don't have a background that would otherwise prohibit them from getting a permit. The bill awaits action from Republican Gov. Dennis Daugaard.*

# CHAPTER TWO

## Evolution of Concealed Permits

The Mississippi Constitution that we currently live by was drafted by Mr. James Zachariah George of Carrollton, Mississippi. He was a Civil War Army Officer, member of the state legislature and eventually a United States Senator. He knew the value of being able to defend one's self. The Mississippi Constitution is sometimes called The Constitution of 1890, for the year it went into effect. Like the US Constitution, over the years, it has undergone changes with revisions and amendments, but as it pertains to our subject of carrying weapons, this is what it says now:

*THE CONSTITUTION OF THE STATE OF MISSISSIPPI*
*ARTICLE 3*
*BILL OF RIGHTS*

*Miss. Const. Ann. Art. 3, § 12 (2011)*

*§ 12. Right to bear arms*

*The right of every citizen to keep and bear arms in defense of his home, person, or property, or in aid of the civil power when thereto legally summoned, shall not be called in question, but the Legislature may regulate or forbid carrying concealed weapons.*

*HISTORY: SOURCES: 1817 art I § 23; 1832 art I § 23; 1869 art I § 15.*

Notice that **bearing arms** is protected (under the constitution). **Concealing arms** is not, and is under the powers given to the legislature.

On March 17, 1886, four years before Mr. George wrote the constitution, a shooting took place directly across the street from his office in the courtroom of the Carroll County Courthouse, on the south side of his office. Over twenty black men were slaughtered because two dared to bring charges against a white lawyer who had himself shot those two on the street near the west side of the courthouse a few weeks before. It started over the two delivering molasses to a saloon for cutting whiskey and the two spilled molasses on the pants of an influential friend of the lawyer. At that time, almost everybody carried handguns. I wrote about this incident in 2010 in a book titled *Blood for Molasses: A Mississippi Massacre*.

I didn't bother to research the previous constitution, but we now know that at least our current Mississippi Constitution grants us the right to "bear" arms. That leaves the legislature to deal with the times and the desires of the people in order to decide whether or not those arms should be concealed. History is important, but only to the extent that it has some bearing on this subject and I will not make any attempt to bog myself down with superfluous research, or bore you with all the changes over the last one hundred or so years. However, I will attempt to shed light on this subject at least back to 1980.

After having been in law enforcement for five years, I left briefly in 1980 to pursue other interests of a security nature in private business. The business had a statewide application. At that time, the Mississippi Highway Patrol issued by law, a "Statewide Gun Permit." This permit was issued if you could show that as a result of your business, you had a need to carry a gun in public, and to carry it into multiple counties necessitating a "Statewide" permit. I received my first Statewide Gun Permit in 1980, signed by David Huggins, Chief Investigator, MHP (now at State Audit).

At that time, it was expected that the local sheriff would arm you if he felt it necessary to carry locally, which sometimes meant that you contributed to his campaign. The permit was often no more than a "Special Deputy" or "Reserve Deputy" card applicable only in that county.

Now, let's fast forward from 1980 through 1990. Effective July 1, 1991, Mississippi had a new law regarding the issuance of permits which was discretionary. The Mississippi Department of Public Safety's discretion in issuing a permit was limited to one area only: if a person had been convicted of "one or more crimes of violence constituting a misdemeanor" in the preceding three years, they were not required to issue a permit, but could issue one if they wanted to do so.

On October 27, 1993 Commissioner Jim Ingram confirmed that his department had issued 7,000 permits since the new law had gone into effect. Based on the state's population at that time .27 (less than one half of one percent) of the population of Mississippi was in possession of concealed weapon permits.

As many as ten to twenty bills having to do with firearms possession were introduced in the Mississippi Legislature each year, over the next several years. The House alone introduced on average, fourteen bills a year with most dying in committee. They ranged from allowing DA investigators to carry weapons, to not allowing weapons where alcohol was served, and even to prevent persons determined to be mentally ill from carrying weapons. Again, most proposed laws or ammendments died on the vine, regardless of how much merit you may think they had.

On July 1, 2004, with the passage of House Bill 989, the Mississippi Department of Public Safety was mandated to issue permits without discretion within 120 days, unless the applicant was found disqualified by virtue of prior disqualifying criminal convictions, etc. We went from a "may issue" state to a "shall issue" state.

Then came the 2005 legislative session. One of my favorites that makes me look back and laugh from that session, was Senate Bill 2289 which would allow Justice Court Judges to carry concealed weapons. Over time, the amendments that allowed other higher court judges to carry weapons seemed to have left them out. The bill did not pass.

The reason I find that humorous though is that in 1977, as a Moss Point Police Officer, myself and fellow officer Wayne Wilson arrested a Justice Court Judge for Carrying a Concealed Weapon. Not only did our city judge rule that he was entitled to carry it, I went on the "black list" for potentially being fired as a trouble-maker based on my efforts.

It all started with Wayne "my pod" (short for partner) arresting a thug on a weapon's charge and Justice Court Judge Swendsen from Escatawpa appearing in our city court as a "character witness" for him. Swendsen appeared in our court carrying a gun himself. Somebody made the comment that Swendsen himself was a convicted felon and it went downhill from there.

A Bureau of Alcohol, Tobacco and Firearms Agent (ATF) from Biloxi suggested that we arrest Swendsen, who regularly paraded around town with a small five-shot .38 Caliber Smith and Wesson revolver on his side.

The ATF agent said he had personally taken Swendsen to federal prison previously on Moonshine charges and provided us a certified copy of Swendsen's conviction. Mississippi statutes did not preclude him from holding office due to his federal conviction.

Swendsen drove through Moss Point at least once a week to hold court at the Jackson County Courthouse in Pascagoula. The agent said he couldn't arrest Swendsen because their law, based on the 1968 Gun Control Act required proof of "receipt" of the gun. They needed a paper that he would have signed saying he wasn't a convicted felon when he bought it.

Wayne, myself and a couple of other young officers were known at the time as the "Mod Squad" after a 1970's TV cop show. We had been given that name by local newspaper reporter Tom Donnely. I didn't think anybody was above the law. The part I was still naive about though was politics, and in that system, the law did not apply to everybody equally. One day Wayne walked into the Chief's office, slammed his ticket book down and said, "why don't you give me a list of people that I CAN arrest?"

It was okay to write a black person or white person that didn't know anybody a ticket. However, the higher class whites that either lived on the west side of town, or had some political connections with the aldermen, mayor, or chief were exempt. Every time we wrote one of them a ticket, it either got torn up, or we got called into the chief's office and told to dismiss it.

We were more aggressive and I thought I was the bravest when it came to my willingness to pursue politicians, but I guess I was the dumbest. That would be proven many times over, as the years ahead made their way behind me.

Anyway, I took on the challenge having seen the judge pass through town a few days before, with a switched tag on his car, which caught my attention with the first letter being an "A" for compact cars. The tag was displayed on a large Chrysler that should have had at least a "C" but probably a "D." It turned out to be a tag from a car he previously owned and had not paid the taxes on the new one. I made arrangements with the dispatcher from the sheriff's office to call our dispatcher when Swendsen left the courtroom. When that happened, Wayne and I positioned ourselves on the highway watching for his car. Within minutes, he came through in his nice new shiny Chrysler with a dirty old tag flopping from a coat hanger wire used to secure it.

I stopped Swendsen on the tag violation that day, backed up by Wayne Wilson. Swendsen got out with the holster on and the gun under the seat. I arrested him and took him to jail. While Wayne and I stood there at the booking window emptying his pockets and frisking him, the Chief of Police walked by. If ever I might have thought I could predict a heart attack, it would have been then. Swendsen himself was rather calm but Chief Charles Barber looked like every ounce of blood had left his body. I thought he would croak at any moment. He didn't, but he did everything he could to make my life miserable from that point on.

God rest his soul, old Captain "Red" Wilson told me I had better find a new job because Charles was going to find a way to fire me. I took Red's advice, although I had already planned to leave anyway.

I was gone in less than a year, but not because of fear from the administration. I found greener pastures and never looked back. I had been shot by the Mayor's brother, dumped on by the City Judge and harassed by the Chief of Police. I didn't want to work in that environment, and I didn't appreciate being put in a situation to have to walk among convicted felons carrying guns.

At any rate, let's move forward to the subject at hand. We know at this point we have a statute not prohibiting us from carrying a weapon, to a statute that allows us to carry, but requiring us to conceal it. However, if we do conceal it, the language defining concealed "in whole or in part" most likely applies.

Sometimes laws are looked at in two ways when we try to interpret them. We might seek to know what the intent of the law is and what the letter of the law is. We think (but aren't sure) the intent of the legislature when they authorized us to carry a concealed weapon is that it should be covered, so as not to be seen without a search.

However, going back to the term "concealed in whole or in part," some police officers have interpreted that to mean even if it is lying on a seat in plain view, it is concealed in part because you can't see the other side. That is a big stretch in my mind, but what if you have it in a holster on your side and have no jacket covering it? Is it not concealed in part with the holster covering the barrel, the cylinder (or frame in the case of a semi-auto) with only the top portion and grip exposed? We know what the letter of the law says, but it will take court cases or future legislative action to clarify the meaning of the law. We may be an "open carry" state and not even know it.

The law keeps changing and the details are sometimes buried in certain bills with their various titles. For instance, i the 2004 session, House Bill number 989 was titled "Weapons permit; revise reciprocity provision." House Bill 506 signed by the governor from the 2011 session which allows us the ability to carry concealed weapons in most places, had that language in a bill titled, "'Weapons Permit; Allow all prosecutors to carry." It allows those of us who complete a course of instruction from a nationally recognized organization that provides firearms instruction, to have an "enhanced carry" endorsement. An endorsement sticker is placed on the back of our regular concealed carry card upon proof of successful course completion.

The laws pertaining to both concealed carry permits and the new enhanced carry (into more public buildings) will be provided next.

The 2010 Senate Bill number 2862 changed a few things that affect all of us who apply for concealed carry permits. The title of that law was "Carrying a concealed weapon; revise qualification for retired law enforcement officers and delete prohibition in parks." However, it did not just pertain to retired law enforcement officers or parks. It did however, transfer the authority of issuing permits for retired policeman to the Police Chief's Association. It is the bill currently displayed on the Mississippi Department of Public Safety's web site and included in the hard copy package they give us upon application. It now limits their time to 45 days in which to act upon an application. It addresses stun guns. It also makes not carrying your permit on your person a non-criminal violation enforceable by citation.

You cannot carry a weapon in:

1. Any police, sheriff or highway patrol station: any detention facility, prison or jail.
2. Any courthouse; any courtroom, except that nothing in this section shall preclude a judge from Carrying a Concealed Weapon or determining who will carry a concealed weapon in his courtroom;
3. Any polling place; any meeting place of the governing body of any governmental entity; any meeting of the Legislature or a committee thereof.
4. Any public park unless for the purpose of participating in any authorized firearms-related activity;
5. Any school, college or professional athletic event not related to firearms;
6. Any portion of an establishment, licensed to dispense alcoholic beverages for consumption on the premises, that is primarily devoted to dispensing alcoholic beverages; any portion of an establishment in which beer or light wine is consumed on the premises, that is primarily devoted to such purpose;
7. Any elementary or secondary school facility; any junior college, community college, college or university facility unless for the purpose of participating in any authorized firearms-related activity;
8. Inside the passenger terminal of any airport, except that no person shall be prohibited from carrying any legal firearm into the terminal if the firearm is encased for shipment, for purposes of checking such firearm as baggage to be lawfully transported on any aircraft;
9. Any church or other place of worship;
10. Or any place where the carrying of firearms is prohibited by federal law.
11. In addition to the places enumerated in this subsection, the carrying of a concealed pistol or revolver may be disallowed in any place in the discretion of the person or entity exercising control over the physical location of such place by the placing of a written notice clearly readable at a distance of not less than ten (10) feet that the "carrying of a pistol or revolver is prohibited."
12. No license issued pursuant to this section shall authorize the participants in a parade or demonstration for which a permit is required to carry a concealed pistol or revolver.

## This bill in it's entirety reads as follows:

SENATE BILL NO. 2862
(As Sent to Governor)

1     AN ACT TO PROVIDE THAT RETIRED LAW ENFORCEMENT OFFICERS MAY
2  BE CERTIFIED BY THE MISSISSIPPI ASSOCIATION OF CHIEFS OF POLICE IN
3  ORDER TO CARRY A CONCEALED WEAPON WITHOUT A PERMIT UNDER FEDERAL
4  LAW; TO AMEND SECTION 45-9-101, MISSISSIPPI CODE OF 1972, TO
5  REMOVE THE PROHIBITION AGAINST CARRYING A WEAPON IN PARKS; AND FOR
6  RELATED PURPOSES.

7     BE IT ENACTED BY THE LEGISLATURE OF THE STATE OF MISSISSIPPI:

8     **SECTION 1.**  (1)  This section may be referred to as the

9  "HR218 Qualification Law."

10     (2)  Any retired law enforcement officer who resides in this

11  state and for whom the law enforcement agency from which the

12  officer retired does not participate in the necessary

13  certification for the retired officer to be certified according to

14  the Law Enforcement Officers Safety Act of 2004 found at Title 18,

15  Chapter 44, Section 926B, USC, or who does not reside in

16  convenient proximity to the law enforcement agency from which the

17  officer retired, may obtain the necessary certification from the

18  Mississippi Association of Chiefs of Police.

19     **SECTION 2.**  Section 45-9-101, Mississippi Code of 1972, is

20  amended as follows:

21     45-9-101.  (1)  (a)  The Department of Public Safety is

22  authorized to issue licenses to carry stun guns, concealed pistols

23  or revolvers to persons qualified as provided in this section.

24  Such licenses shall be valid throughout the state for a period of

25  five (5) years from the date of issuance.  Any person possessing a

26  valid license issued pursuant to this section may carry a stun

27  gun, concealed pistol or concealed revolver.

28          (b)   The licensee must carry the license, together with

29   valid identification, at all times in which the licensee is

30   carrying a stun gun, concealed pistol or revolver and must display

31   both the license and proper identification upon demand by a law

32   enforcement officer.  A violation of the provisions of this

33   paragraph (b) shall constitute a noncriminal violation with a

34   penalty of Twenty-five Dollars ($25.00) and shall be enforceable

35   by summons.

36      (2)   The Department of Public Safety shall issue a license if

37   the applicant:

38          (a)   Is a resident of the state and has been a resident

39   for twelve (12) months or longer immediately preceding the filing

40   of the application.  However, this residency requirement may be

41   waived, provided the applicant possesses a valid permit from

42   another state, is active military personnel stationed in

43   Mississippi or is a retired law enforcement officer establishing

44   residency in the state;

45          (b)   Is twenty-one (21) years of age or older;

46          (c)   Does not suffer from a physical infirmity which

47   prevents the safe handling of a stun gun, pistol or revolver;

48          (d)   Is not ineligible to possess a firearm by virtue of

49   having been convicted of a felony in a court of this state, of any

50   other state, or of the United States without having been pardoned

51   for same;

52          (e)   Does not chronically or habitually abuse controlled

53   substances to the extent that his normal faculties are impaired.

54   It shall be presumed that an applicant chronically and habitually

55   uses controlled substances to the extent that his faculties are

56   impaired if the applicant has been voluntarily or involuntarily

57   committed to a treatment facility for the abuse of a controlled

58   substance or been found guilty of a crime under the provisions of

59   the Uniform Controlled Substances Law or similar laws of any other

60   state or the United States relating to controlled substances

61   within a three-year period immediately preceding the date on which
62   the application is submitted;

63          (f)   Does not chronically and habitually use alcoholic
64   beverages to the extent that his normal faculties are impaired.
65   It shall be presumed that an applicant chronically and habitually
66   uses alcoholic beverages to the extent that his normal faculties
67   are impaired if the applicant has been voluntarily or
68   involuntarily committed as an alcoholic to a treatment facility or
69   has been convicted of two (2) or more offenses related to the use
70   of alcohol under the laws of this state or similar laws of any
71   other state or the United States within the three-year period
72   immediately preceding the date on which the application is
73   submitted;

74          (g)   Desires a legal means to carry a stun gun,
75   concealed pistol or revolver to defend himself;

76          (h)   Has not been adjudicated mentally incompetent, or
77   has waited five (5) years from the date of his restoration to
78   capacity by court order;

79          (i)   Has not been voluntarily or involuntarily committed
80   to a mental institution or mental health treatment facility unless
81   he possesses a certificate from a psychiatrist licensed in this
82   state that he has not suffered from disability for a period of
83   five (5) years;

84          (j)   Has not had adjudication of guilt withheld or
85   imposition of sentence suspended on any felony unless three (3)
86   years have elapsed since probation or any other conditions set by
87   the court have been fulfilled;

88          (k)   Is not a fugitive from justice; and

89          (l)   Is not disqualified to possess or own a weapon
90   based on federal law.

91      (3)   The Department of Public Safety may deny a license if
92   the applicant has been found guilty of one or more crimes of
93   violence constituting a misdemeanor unless three (3) years have

94 elapsed since probation or any other conditions set by the court
95 have been fulfilled or expunction has occurred prior to the date
96 on which the application is submitted, or may revoke a license if
97 the licensee has been found guilty of one or more crimes of
98 violence within the preceding three (3) years. The department
99 shall, upon notification by a law enforcement agency or a court
100 and subsequent written verification, suspend a license or the
101 processing of an application for a license if the licensee or
102 applicant is arrested or formally charged with a crime which would
103 disqualify such person from having a license under this section,
104 until final disposition of the case. The provisions of subsection
105 (7) of this section shall apply to any suspension or revocation of
106 a license pursuant to the provisions of this section.
107     (4) The application shall be completed, under oath, on a
108 form promulgated by the Department of Public Safety and shall
109 include only:
110         (a) The name, address, place and date of birth, race,
111 sex and occupation of the applicant;
112         (b) The driver's license number or social security
113 number of applicant;
114         (c) Any previous address of the applicant for the two
115 (2) years preceding the date of the application;
116         (d) A statement that the applicant is in compliance
117 with criteria contained within subsections (2) and (3) of this
118 section;
119         (e) A statement that the applicant has been furnished a
120 copy of this section and is knowledgeable of its provisions;
121         (f) A conspicuous warning that the application is
122 executed under oath and that a knowingly false answer to any
123 question, or the knowing submission of any false document by the
124 applicant, subjects the applicant to criminal prosecution; and

125          (g)  A statement that the applicant desires a legal
126    means to carry a stun gun, concealed pistol or revolver to defend
127    himself.
128          (5)  The applicant shall submit only the following to the
129    Department of Public Safety:
130          (a)  A completed application as described in subsection
131    (4) of this section;
132          (b)  A full-face photograph of the applicant taken
133    within the preceding thirty (30) days in which the head, including
134    hair, in a size as determined by the Department of Public Safety;
135          (c)  A nonrefundable license fee of One Hundred Dollars
136    ($100.00).  Costs for processing the set of fingerprints as
137    required in paragraph (d) of this subsection shall be borne by the
138    applicant.  Honorably retired law enforcement officers shall be
139    exempt from the payment of the license fee;
140          (d)  A full set of fingerprints of the applicant
141    administered by the Department of Public Safety; and
142          (e)  A waiver authorizing the Department of Public
143    Safety access to any records concerning commitments of the
144    applicant to any of the treatment facilities or institutions
145    referred to in subsection (2) and permitting access to all the
146    applicant's criminal records.
147    (6)  (a)  The Department of Public Safety, upon receipt of
148    the items listed in subsection (5) of this section, shall forward
149    the full set of fingerprints of the applicant to the appropriate
150    agencies for state and federal processing.
151          (b)  The Department of Public Safety shall forward a
152    copy of the applicant's application to the sheriff of the
153    applicant's county of residence and, if applicable, the police
154    chief of the applicant's municipality of residence.  The sheriff
155    of the applicant's county of residence and, if applicable, the
156    police chief of the applicant's municipality of residence may, at
157    his discretion, participate in the process by submitting a

158  voluntary report to the Department of Public Safety containing any
159  readily discoverable prior information that he feels may be
160  pertinent to the licensing of any applicant.  The reporting shall
161  be made within thirty (30) days after the date he receives the
162  copy of the application.  Upon receipt of a response from a
163  sheriff or police chief, such sheriff or police chief shall be
164  reimbursed at a rate set by the department.
165          (c)  The Department of Public Safety shall, within
166  forty-five (45) days after the date of receipt of the items listed
167  in subsection (5) of this section:
168              (i)  Issue the license;
169              (ii)  Deny the application based solely on the
170  ground that the applicant fails to qualify under the criteria
171  listed in subsections (2) and (3) of this section.  If the
172  Department of Public Safety denies the application, it shall
173  notify the applicant in writing, stating the ground for denial,
174  and the denial shall be subject to the appeal process set forth in
175  subsection (7); or
176              (iii)  Notify the applicant that the department is
177  unable to make a determination regarding the issuance or denial of
178  a license within the forty-five-day period prescribed by this
179  subsection, and provide an estimate of the amount of time the
180  department will need to make the determination.
181          (d)  In the event a legible set of fingerprints, as
182  determined by the Department of Public Safety and the Federal
183  Bureau of Investigation, cannot be obtained after a minimum of two
184  (2) attempts, the Department of Public Safety shall determine
185  eligibility based upon a name check by the Mississippi Highway
186  Safety Patrol and a Federal Bureau of Investigation name check
187  conducted by the Mississippi Highway Safety Patrol at the request
188  of the Department of Public Safety.
189      (7)  (a)  If the Department of Public Safety denies the
190  issuance of a license, or suspends or revokes a license, the party

191    aggrieved may appeal such denial, suspension or revocation to the

192    Commissioner of Public Safety, or his authorized agent, within

193    thirty (30) days after the aggrieved party receives written notice

194    of such denial, suspension or revocation.  The Commissioner of

195    Public Safety, or his duly authorized agent, shall rule upon such

196    appeal within thirty (30) days after the appeal is filed and

197    failure to rule within this thirty-day period shall constitute

198    sustaining such denial, suspension or revocation.  Such review

199    shall be conducted pursuant to such reasonable rules and

200    regulations as the Commissioner of Public Safety may adopt.

201            (b)  If the revocation, suspension or denial of issuance

202    is sustained by the Commissioner of Public Safety, or his duly

203    authorized agent pursuant to paragraph (a) of this subsection, the

204    aggrieved party may file within ten (10) days after the rendition

205    of such decision a petition in the circuit or county court of his

206    residence for review of such decision.  A hearing for review shall

207    be held and shall proceed before the court without a jury upon the

208    record made at the hearing before the Commissioner of Public

209    Safety or his duly authorized agent.  No such party shall be

210    allowed to carry a stun gun, concealed pistol or revolver pursuant

211    to the provisions of this section while any such appeal is

212    pending.

213            (8)  The Department of Public Safety shall maintain an

214    automated listing of license holders and such information shall be

215    available online, upon request, at all times, to all law

216    enforcement agencies through the Mississippi Crime Information

217    Center.  However, the records of the department relating to

218    applications for licenses to carry stun guns, concealed pistols or

219    revolvers and records relating to license holders shall be exempt

220    from the provisions of the Mississippi Public Records Act of 1983

221    for a period of forty-five (45) days from the date of the issuance

222    of the license or the final denial of an application.

223      (9)  Within thirty (30) days after the changing of a
224  permanent address, or within thirty (30) days after having a
225  license lost or destroyed, the licensee shall notify the
226  Department of Public Safety in writing of such change or loss.
227  Failure to notify the Department of Public Safety pursuant to the
228  provisions of this subsection shall constitute a noncriminal
229  violation with a penalty of Twenty-five Dollars ($25.00) and shall
230  be enforceable by a summons.

231      (10)  In the event that a stun gun, concealed pistol or
232  revolver license is lost or destroyed, the person to whom the
233  license was issued shall comply with the provisions of subsection
234  (9) of this section and may obtain a duplicate, or substitute
235  thereof, upon payment of Fifteen Dollars ($15.00) to the
236  Department of Public Safety, and furnishing a notarized statement
237  to the department that such license has been lost or destroyed.

238      (11)  A license issued under this section shall be revoked if
239  the licensee becomes ineligible under the criteria set forth in
240  subsection (2) of this section.

241      (12)  (a)  No less than ninety (90) days prior to the
242  expiration date of the license, the Department of Public Safety
243  shall mail to each licensee a written notice of the expiration and
244  a renewal form prescribed by the department.  The licensee must
245  renew his license on or before the expiration date by filing with
246  the department the renewal form, a notarized affidavit stating
247  that the licensee remains qualified pursuant to the criteria
248  specified in subsections (2) and (3) of this section, and a full
249  set of fingerprints administered by the Department of Public
250  Safety or the sheriff of the county of residence of the licensee.
251  The first renewal may be processed by mail and the subsequent
252  renewal must be made in person.  Thereafter every other renewal
253  may be processed by mail to assure that the applicant must appear
254  in person every ten (10) years for the purpose of obtaining a new
255  photograph.

256                     (i)   Except as provided in this subsection, a
257   renewal fee of Fifty Dollars ($50.00) shall also be submitted
258   along with costs for processing the fingerprints;
259                     (ii)   Honorably retired law enforcement officers
260   shall be exempt from the renewal fee; and
261                     (iii)   The renewal fee for a Mississippi resident
262   aged sixty-five (65) years of age or older shall be Twenty-five
263   Dollars ($25.00).
264             (b)   The Department of Public Safety shall forward the
265   full set of fingerprints of the applicant to the appropriate
266   agencies for state and federal processing.   The license shall be
267   renewed upon receipt of the completed renewal application and
268   appropriate payment of fees.
269             (c)   A licensee who fails to file a renewal application
270   on or before its expiration date must renew his license by paying
271   a late fee of Fifteen Dollars ($15.00).   No license shall be
272   renewed six (6) months or more after its expiration date, and such
273   license shall be deemed to be permanently expired.   A person whose
274   license has been permanently expired may reapply for licensure;
275   however, an application for licensure and fees pursuant to
276   subsection (5) of this section must be submitted, and a background
277   investigation shall be conducted pursuant to the provisions of
278   this section.
279         (13)   No license issued pursuant to this section shall
280   authorize any person to carry a stun gun, concealed pistol or
281   revolver into any place of nuisance as defined in Section 95-3-1,
282   Mississippi Code of 1972; any police, sheriff or highway patrol
283   station; any detention facility, prison or jail; any courthouse;
284   any courtroom, except that nothing in this section shall preclude
285   a judge from carrying a concealed weapon or determining who will
286   carry a concealed weapon in his courtroom; any polling place; any
287   meeting place of the governing body of any governmental entity;
288   any meeting of the Legislature or a committee thereof; * * * any

289 school, college or professional athletic event not related to
290 firearms; any portion of an establishment, licensed to dispense
291 alcoholic beverages for consumption on the premises, that is
292 primarily devoted to dispensing alcoholic beverages; any portion
293 of an establishment in which beer or light wine is consumed on the
294 premises, that is primarily devoted to such purpose; any
295 elementary or secondary school facility; any junior college,
296 community college, college or university facility unless for the
297 purpose of participating in any authorized firearms-related
298 activity; inside the passenger terminal of any airport, except
299 that no person shall be prohibited from carrying any legal firearm
300 into the terminal if the firearm is encased for shipment, for
301 purposes of checking such firearm as baggage to be lawfully
302 transported on any aircraft; any church or other place of worship;
303 or any place where the carrying of firearms is prohibited by
304 federal law.  In addition to the places enumerated in this
305 subsection, the carrying of a stun gun, concealed pistol or
306 revolver may be disallowed in any place in the discretion of the
307 person or entity exercising control over the physical location of
308 such place by the placing of a written notice clearly readable at
309 a distance of not less than ten (10) feet that the "carrying of a
310 pistol or revolver is prohibited." No license issued pursuant to
311 this section shall authorize the participants in a parade or
312 demonstration for which a permit is required to carry a stun gun,
313 concealed pistol or revolver.

314     (14) A law enforcement officer as defined in Section 45-6-3,
315 chiefs of police, sheriffs and persons licensed as professional
316 bondsmen pursuant to Chapter 39, Title 83, Mississippi Code of
317 1972, shall be exempt from the licensing requirements of this
318 section.

319     (15) Any person who knowingly submits a false answer to any
320 question on an application for a license issued pursuant to this
321 section, or who knowingly submits a false document when applying

322  for a license issued pursuant to this section, shall, upon

323  conviction, be guilty of a misdemeanor and shall be punished as

324  provided in Section 99-19-31, Mississippi Code of 1972.

325       (16)  All fees collected by the Department of Public Safety

326  pursuant to this section shall be deposited into a special fund

327  hereby created in the State Treasury and shall be used for

328  implementation and administration of this section.  After the

329  close of each fiscal year, the balance in this fund shall be

330  certified to the Legislature and then may be used by the

331  Department of Public Safety as directed by the Legislature.

332       (17)  All funds received by a sheriff or police chief

333  pursuant to the provisions of this section shall be deposited into

334  the general fund of the county or municipality, as appropriate,

335  and shall be budgeted to the sheriff's office or police department

336  as appropriate.

337       (18)  Nothing in this section shall be construed to require

338  or allow the registration, documentation or providing of serial

339  numbers with regard to any stun gun or firearm.  Further, nothing

340  in this section shall be construed to allow the open and

341  unconcealed carrying of any stun gun or a deadly weapon as

342  described in Section 97-37-1, Mississippi Code of 1972.

343       (19)  Any person holding a valid unrevoked and unexpired

344  license to carry stun guns, concealed pistols or revolvers issued

345  in another state shall have such license recognized by this state

346  to carry stun guns, concealed pistols or revolvers, provided that

347  the issuing state authorizes license holders from this state to

348  carry stun guns, concealed pistols or revolvers in such issuing

349  state and the appropriate authority has communicated that fact to

350  the Department of Public Safety.

351       (20)  The provisions of this section shall be under the

352  supervision of the Commissioner of Public Safety.  The

353  commissioner is authorized to promulgate reasonable rules and

354  regulations to carry out the provisions of this section.

```
355        (21)  For the purposes of this section, the term "stun gun"
356   means a portable device or weapon from which an electric current,
357   impulse, wave or beam may be directed, which current, impulse,
358   wave or beam is designed to incapacitate temporarily, injure,
359   momentarily stun, knock out, cause mental disorientation or
360   paralyze.
361        SECTION 3.  This act shall take effect and be in force from
362   and after July 1, 2010.
```

Before reading the above bill, I pointed out to you the places you were not allowed to go with a concealed weapon. Well, the following year in the 2011 session, House Bill 506 went further than that.

This bill went into effect in July 2011 and gave more authority for permit holders to carry guns in places prohibited in the previous legislation, with the stipulation that those seeking the "enhanced carry" authorization receive certain training.

The responsibility to determine instructor qualifications and the course curriculum was placed on the Mississippi Highway Patrol (MHP). For several months, no agreement was reached. However, it was later determined that the Concealed Weapons Permit Division of the Mississippi Highway Patrol would approve instructors based on their credentials. The instructors would conduct training with an agreement between them and the patrol by virtue of a Memorandum of Understanding (MOU). The instructors would make their own arrangements with students. Once trained, the students would obtain a sticker from MPH for the back of their concealed weapon permit, as an endorsement. The pertinent section of that bill follows:

*A person licensed under Section 45-9-101 to carry a concealed pistol, who has voluntarily completed an instructional course in the safe handling and use of firearms offered by an instructor certified by a nationally recognized organization that customarily offers firearms training, or by any other organization approved by the Department of Public Safety, shall also be authorized to carry weapons in courthouses except in courtrooms during a judicial proceeding, and any location listed in subsection (13) of Section 97 45-9-101, except any place of nuisance as defined in Section 98 95-3-1, any police, sheriff or highway patrol station or any detention facility, prison or jail. The department shall promulgate rules and regulations allowing concealed pistol permit holders to obtain an endorsement on their permit indicating that they have completed the aforementioned course and have the authority to carry in these locations.*

To obtain a copy of the Concealed Weapon Permit application package, go to this website address: http://www.dps.state.ms.us/

Click on the FIREARMS PERMIT UNIT tab on the left side of the screen. Click on the words "Individual Permit" highlighted in blue near the bottom in the center of the screen. If you get confused or need additional information, the phone numbers for help are displayed there.

Fees
1st Time Individual * $100.00
Fingerprint/Background Check Processing $32.00
Renewal * $50.00
65 or Older * $25.00
Duplicate $15.00
Late Renewal $15.00 (extra)

To find an approved instructor that can train you for the enhanced carry, once you have clicked on the FIREARMS PERMIT UNIT tab, click on ENHANCED PERMIT CERTIFIED FIREARMS INSTRUCTORS. Find one in your area, contact him for prices and schedules.

# CHAPTER THREE

## Laws Associated with Weapons Use

Before you decide to go out and buy a gun to conceal on your person, you need to really understand justifiable reasons for using that weapon. You may have a gun and you may know how to shoot it, but you still may be a little fuzzy on when to use it in a situation that may take another person's life. Police officers in many jurisdictions receive extensive training in judgmental shooting, often using electronic "shoot-don't shoot" scenarios played on video devices. More will be said on that subject later.

Since you are most likely a civilian not authorized to carry a weapon in the performance of your public duties, you may have had no exposure to laws that may become familiar to you as a result of shooting. You won't be responding to robberies or burglaries, or even assaults on other persons as a civilian. However, you may happen to be in the wrong place at the wrong time and have to make a snap decision as to how to handle this situation. That is going to be up to your own judgment. You should be well informed on the law before exercising that judgment.

In 2008 in Jackson, Mississippi a man was pursued into the parking lot by a store owner and shot to death for stealing and running away with a case of beer. This incident was reported by the local press with headlines calling it a robbery. Based on the facts reported at the time, it was a larceny, not a robbery. Larcenies fall into at least two categories and will be discussed later. The store owner was charged with murder for taking a life over a misdemeanor incident (theft of property valued at under $500).

However, the Jackson media reported On November 11, 2010 that a Hinds county jury of ten blacks and two whites found the shooter (an Indian) not guilty in the murder of a 36 year old black male. In closing arguments the shooter's defense attorneyr said his client feared for his life when he saw the black male reaching for what he thought was a gun. The attorney told reporters leaving the courtroom, "I think this verdict sends the message that people are tired of the crime, they are saying stop the robbing, stop the stealing." The deceased's mother said, "Everyone can go get a gun, it will be like the Wild West!"

A white pharmacist in Oklahoma City shot and killed a sixteen year old black male during a robbery gone bad. It was clearly a robbery as caught on video tape with the robber shooting at the pharmacist when he declined to hand over money and drugs. The young man was accompanied by another young black male who escaped but was later caught. More details to follow.

First let's look at Mississippi laws on Larceny. The first law we will discuss is Grand Larceny:

*§ 97-17-41. Grand larceny*

*(1) Every person who shall be convicted of taking and carrying away, feloniously, the personal property of another, of the value of Five Hundred Dollars ($ 500.00) or more, shall be guilty of grand larceny, and shall be imprisoned in the Penitentiary for a term not exceeding ten (10) years; or shall be fined not more than Ten Thousand Dollars ($ 10,000.00), or both. The total value of property taken and carried away by the person from a single victim shall be aggregated in determining the gravity of the offense.*

Clearly a case of beer is not worth more than $500 so the thief (not robber) who fled with however much beer he had, did not have $500 worth. There are probably bottles of wine held in special reserves that are worth that much, but not beer found in our convenience stores. However, the key to the case mentioned is the lawyer (not the defendant who remained silent) told the jury his client had seen what he "thought" was the thief going for a gun and therefore was "placed in fear of his life." That is what saved him from a murder conviction, along with, as the lawyer said, Jacksonians were tired of the crime and sending a message. See the "Petit Larceny" statute below:

*§ 97-17-43. Petit larceny defined; penalty*

(1) If **any person shall feloniously take, steal and carry away any personal property of another under the value of Five Hundred Dollars ($ 500.00), he shall be guilty of petit larceny** and, upon conviction, shall be punished by imprisonment in the county jail not exceeding six (6) months or by fine not exceeding One Thousand Dollars ($ 1,000.00), or both.

*Total value of property taken, stolen or carried away by the person from a single victim shall be aggregated in determining the gravity of the offense.*

The beer snatcher was a petty thief, not a dangerous felon (who might have placed the storeowner in fear of his life later). But did the jury understand that the clerk "thought" he saw a gun inside the store, or was it after he chased him into the parking lot? If he was in fear of his life would he have chased the thief outside...would it have mattered? Did the "Castle Law" protect the store owner? More on that later.

Now let's take a look at robbery which does not distinguish between the values of the money taken although recently a couple was released from years of prison time after they made light of the fact that they only got a few dollars (after the man was robbed at gunpoint and beaten). You can take one thing to the bank. If the victim had been found to have thousands of dollars on him at the time, the assailants would not have only taken a few dollars. I think that case was a farce. At any rate, here's what Mississippi statutes say about robbery:

*§ 97-3-73. Robbery; definition*

*Every person who **shall feloniously take the personal property of another, in his presence or from his person and against his will, by violence to his person or by putting such person in fear of some immediate injury** to his person, shall be guilty of robbery.*

The bold text above is the clear distinction between larceny and robbery. If somebody grabs something of yours and runs away with it, you fear losing that property but probably are not in fear of harm by the person since they are running away. They may even steal from you without you even knowing they were there or the item is even missing. Again, that is larceny. But robbing, or attempting to rob the pharmacist is a whole new ball game. The penalty is described next.

*§ 97-3-75. Robbery; penalty*

*Every person convicted of robbery shall be punished by imprisonment in the penitentiary for a term not more than fifteen years.*

The judge has a great deal of discretion in determining the amount of punishment. It could be based on the person's past record and/or based on the circumstances at the time of the robbery, whether it was with a weapon or without (can be done by handing a note, or threatening a family member). It could be called "strong armed robbery" or "armed robbery." Both are felonies and considered crimes against persons, not crimes against property like larceny is. The circumstances at the time and whether or not anyone was injured are all factors that allow the judge to award up to fifteen years.

## JUSTIFICATION

Now before we go further, and look at the Oklahoma pharmacist shooting and the Mississippi store clerk shooting, it is important for us to look at the real issue at hand. That is, whether or not either of the men were justified in what they did. Let's pose this question, "did they use force likely to result in serious or grievous bodily harm?" In other words, did they strike their offenders with a rubber baseball bat, or a high-speed metal projectile capable of taking another person's life? Clearly, both of them used that force likely to result in death and it did in both cases. So the next question at hand is, "did they have the authority by law to do what they did?"

To find that answer, let's look at Mississippi law on the use of force: (We will address the term "duty to retreat" seen below later.)

*§ 97-3-15. Homicide; justifiable homicide; use of defensive force; duty to retreat*

*(e) When committed by any person in resisting any attempt unlawfully to kill such person or to commit any felony upon him, or upon or in any dwelling, in any occupied vehicle, in any place of business, in any place of employment or in the immediate premises thereof in which such person shall be;*

*(f) When committed in the lawful defense of one's own person or any other human being, where there shall be reasonable ground to apprehend a design to commit a felony or to do some great personal injury, and there shall be imminent danger of such design being accomplished;*

If the reasonable man doctrine were used, any "reasonable person" might have concluded that neither of the above defenses of justification for homicide fits the store clerk shooting the beer thief. The offender did not attempt to kill the store clerk, nor did he commit a felony. His running away, clearly shows there was no attempt to inflict personal injury or place the clerk in imminent danger AT THAT TIME. (Unless new information appears that shows the clerk was somehow placed in fear of his life.)

On the other hand, a closer look at the pharmacist reveals information previously unknown to you, the reader, unless you are familiar with it from the media. The fact is, the pharmacist was a victim of each of the descriptions listed in paragraph (e) and (f) of Section 97-3-15. The robber was shooting at him and one could reasonably argue, in an attempt to kill him. The robber was also committing a felony at the risk of personal injury and placing the pharmacist in imminent danger. So he was completely justified in killing the youngster right?

The District Attorney says, "no" and indicted the man for murder. What I didn't tell you, was withheld so as to address another factor required in the use of force even in our state of Mississippi. The pharmacist shot the man in the head and his weapon slid down the isle, out of his reach as he lay bleeding and injured, no longer posing a threat. The pharmacist then briefly pursued the accomplice out the door to no avail. However, he returned and as his own video surveillance camera was running, pumped five more rounds into the robber's body which killed him. The District Attorney said the head wound was not a grave injury and the deceased would likely have lived.

Now let's look at the other element of the law.

*(3) A person who uses defensive force shall be presumed to have reasonably feared imminent death or great bodily harm, or the commission of a felony upon him or another or upon his dwelling, or against a vehicle which he was occupying, or against his business or place of employment or the immediate premises of such business or place of employment, if the person against whom the defensive force was used, was in the process of unlawfully and forcibly entering, or had unlawfully and forcibly entered, a dwelling, occupied vehicle, business, place of employment or the immediate premises thereof or if that person had unlawfully removed or was attempting to unlawfully remove another against the other person's will from that dwelling, occupied vehicle, business, place of employment or the immediate premises thereof and the person who used defensive force knew or had reason to believe that the forcible entry or unlawful and forcible act was occurring or had occurred.*

The facts in this case show the pharmacist left the building knowing his robber was down, injured and disarmed. He turned his back on the robber and pursued the accomplice out of the building. He returned finding the robber as he left him, on the floor in a prone position, bleeding, injured, incapacitated, disarmed, not attempting to run or put up a fight, and instead of holding the gun on him and calling 911, he pumped five more rounds into the center of his body, terminating all signs of life.

This pharmacist was convicted of murder on May 26, 2011 and sentenced July 12, 2011 to life in prison. I had no doubt he would have had a hard time convincing a jury that those last five rounds were fired as defensive force at a time when this incapacitated person could not have placed him in further fear for his life. He appeared to be an executioner who played judge and jury. That's just my opinion. Check it out on You tube if you want to form your own opinion. But remember, Oklahoma's laws are not the same as Mississippi's. We will be discussing another Oklahoma scenario later so you will be able to see the difference in the circumstances.

That brings me to my responsibility for telling you about "duty to retreat." The pharmacist could have chosen to run out the back door (if there was one), or maybe could have just given up the money and drugs, even abandoning the store and giving it to the robbers to do what they wanted. That action would have been known as a "retreat." Some states require you to attempt to retreat if that is possible. Here is what current Mississippi law says in the same statute about that requirement to retreat:

*4) A **person who is not the initial aggressor and is not engaged in unlawful activity shall have <u>no duty to retreat</u> before using deadly force** under subsection (1) (e) or (f) of this section **if the person is in a place where the person has a right to be,** and no finder of fact shall be permitted to consider the person's failure to retreat as evidence that the person's use of force was unnecessary, excessive or unreasonable.*

## PROTECTION OF HOME AND FAMILY

Another recent case along these lines that I would like to mention is an Oklahoma case where a young mother who had recently lost her husband to cancer was being harassed by a man that she feared. She saw him out the window of her house approaching with another man. She called 911 and asked if she could shoot, if they broke into her house. The 911 dispatcher fell short of authorizing her to shoot but told her she should do whatever was necessary to protect herself and her baby if they broke in. She raised a twelve gauge double barrel shotgun towards the door and held a pistol under it. One of the suspects had a large hunting knife. As they broke through the door, she fired the shotgun killing one suspect while the other fled.

The District Attorney ruled it justifiable homicide, but noted that in Oklahoma, the law required that the suspect be inside her home through the use of force. However, I would like to make another interesting point about both the pharmacist and the young girl's assailants. Both had accomplices that escaped and since their involvement in the crimes led to the death of another, both accomplices were charged with murder.

## RECOGNIZING A NON-THREAT

When I was a child, a young man who lived next to us fell asleep while driving home, and had an accident while his arm was resting in the driver's window, allowing smoke from his cigarette to drift outside. He ran off the road and hit a series of trees on the driver's side. It was late at night and he staggered onto our porch, pushing the door open in need of medical attention. He had so much blood on his face he was unrecognizable. Blood in his mouth and throat prevented him from speaking.

An unrecognizable, bloody man busting through the door of your home at night would probably scare the hell out of the average person, enough so to cause a prudent man to be in fear of his life and shoot the person. I am sure the only reason my dad didn't, was that he didn't have his gun on his person at the time and didn't have enough time to get it. Luckily he didn't and we took the young man to the hospital when we figured out who he was, and what had happened.

## SELF DEFENSE ISSUE

Another case with a different twist involved a nephew of mine a few years ago. He had been seriously injured in several accidents and was drawing social security. He was considered totally disabled.

His neck had been broken and pinned back together. He was taking insulin shots, and had been for several years, for diabetes. He was obese and had high blood pressure among several other medical issues. He didn't feel he could adequately protect himself, so he obtained a concealed carry permit years ago.

He went to a bar one night and left his gun under his truck seat. While inside, he met and spoke with a young lady. What has been described as a former acquaintance of hers confronted my nephew and words were exchanged over the girl. Eventually my nephew decided to leave.

He went out into the dark parking lot and was about to leave. He said he opened his door to get inside and somebody struck him in the back at the base of his neck causing him to fall onto the truck seat face down, in front of the steering wheel.

The attacker continued to beat him in the back until he was out of breath. My nephew said all he could think of was his neck breaking again because his doctor had said a blow in that area, could paralyze him.

As luck would have it, while lying face down on the seat, his left hand was in the floorboard only inches from the gun under the seat. He grabbed the gun, rolled over, and fired a shot that either missed, or slightly wounded the assailant who kept coming at him. He fired another shot into the attacker's neck and the attacker went down.

My nephew used good judgment when he stopped firing after the suspect no longer posed a threat to him even though he was still alive.

My nephew was arrested and charged with aggravated assault, probably because of where it happened. He went to court and testified that he was in fear of his life, that the young man could have broken his neck resulting in paralysis and maybe death, so he defended himself with his gun. Unfortunately for the assailant, he was the one paralyzed and my nephew was found not guilty very quickly by the jury.

Another interesting case involving self-defense, fear of life, Castle Doctrine and so on, is one that happened in Pasadena, Texas in 2007. The Castle Doctrine applies when a man is protecting his home (HIS being the operative word). In this case, a homeowner argued with the 911 dispatcher on the phone that the burglars were about to get away and he had to protect himself. The dispatcher insisted no property was worth killing somebody over and that police were on their way. The caller refused to listen and told the dispatcher the law had changed that previous September and he was going to defend his rights. He insisted that the 911 dispatcher listen to the sound of his shotgun as he shot the burglars. The dispatcher kept saying, "no."

The burglars were both illegal immigrants from Columbia. Both were shot in the back. Horn fired thee times. The real issue was whether or not the Castle Law applied to the legal right of protecting a neighbor's house and whether or not Horn was in fear of his life. The police would let the grand jury decide.

The grand jury, whether loosely interpreting the Castle Law, or just plain sick and tired of criminals getting away with their crimes, chose not to indict the shooter. Their very presence in the country was a crime.

ABC Nightline, June 30, 2008 quoted the District Attorney as sayin, The use of deadly force is carefully limited in Texas law to certain circumstances. ... In this case, however, the grand jury concluded that (the shooter's) use of deadly force did not rise to a criminal offense."

I won't attempt to provide all the potential statutes in their entirety. However, I will provide you with the web address where you can search the statutes and I will provide you the section numbers and titles of those likely to result in armed conflict. To access the website go to:

http://www.lexisnexis.com/hottopics/mscode/

*§ 97-3-7. Simple assault; aggravated assault; simple domestic violence; aggravated domestic violence*

*§ 97-3-15. Homicide; justifiable homicide; use of defensive force; duty to retreat*

*§ 97-37-19. Deadly weapons; exhibiting in rude, angry, or threatening manner*

*§ 97-3-117. Mississippi Carjacking Act; what constitutes offense of carjacking; attempted carjacking; armed carjacking; penalties*

*§ 97-17-23. Burglary; breaking and entering inhabited dwelling; home invasion*

*§ 97-17-33. Burglary; breaking and entering building other than dwelling; railroad car; vessels; automobiles*

*§ 97-17-51. Larceny; stealing dog*

*§ 97-17-67. Malicious mischief*

*97-23-93. Shoplifting; elements of offense; presumptions; evidence; penalties; aggregation of multiple offenses occurring within same jurisdiction over 30-day period in determining gravity of offense*

I recommend you go to the site and read each of the above statutes in their entirety since they are too voluminous to include in this book. However, keep in mind, this is not an all inclusive list.

# CHAPTER FOUR

## Facts/Misconceptions on Shooting

There is no question you will need to know how to aim a weapon. You will be taught what the rear site picture looks like, the front sight picture, the two together and how they are properly aligned on the target. However, the need to aim in most shoot situations, especially those you might be unlucky enough to be in, is slim to none.

Police officers are accustomed to responding to dangerous calls. They know how to take precautions and approach a scene with extreme care. For that reason they keep their distance whenever possible. They take cover.

They make themselves look smaller than they are at times by ducking down, turning sideways, and so forth. You are most likely just an "average Joe" going about your daily life without expecting everybody you come into contact with to shoot you. In most cases anybody that will want to shoot you, or someone else, will already be within arm's reach of you. There most likely will be no time to think, aim, stand correctly, regulate your breathing or maintain proper control of the weapon, including trigger control. There rarely is for police officers either, and they expect it.

A person that intends to shoot you, has already made his or her mind up. That puts them in the offensive (ready) position and you will have to see, and recognize the threat before you respond to defend yourself. So you see the weapon in the person's hand. There is a time lapse before your eyes and brain work together to tell you that you have a problem. Then there is a time lapse of however long it takes you to draw your weapon (point or aim), then fire. In most cases you are already dead. Maybe not if you take cover.

The FBI compiles a report each year that outlines all the details of police shootings when officers die. Other large agencies have from time to time conducted their own studies. I have conducted my own, using a firearms simulator.

Some of the things we like to know in order to adjust our training include, distance from the shooter, hit probability, whether or not sights were used, and what other phenomena the officer may have experienced before, during and after the shooting.

There are those law enforcement professionals and instructors that swear by sights. There are also those who don't. Rather than get into an argument with either one, I will just show you what you are likely to come into contact with, and you can practice both techniques to determine which is best for you. Before I do though, I will make this statement. *Precise shot placement is the number one action that will save your life, so accuracy is very important.* However, in order to become very accurate in a training environment, you have to practice, practice and practice some more. Most of us don't have the time, or money for ammunition to practice to the degree that we become that proficient. If you have that much time and money, by all means, do it.

The truth is though, outside the training environment, few things happen the way you expect them to, and the methods you would like to employ for the ideal shot are often impossible. Most of your actions in real-life will be "point and shoot" whether you intended that or not. You may not even remember if you used sights, or how many shots you or your adversary fired. You may not ever be able to assume the stance you were taught. Your breathing may become very erratic; your hands may begin to shake. It has been my experience that if you are far enough away that you need sights, you are far enough away to take evasive action, or the suspect may well run away.

A weapon in your hand is an extension of your arm. If you can point, you can shoot at that point in many cases without sights if your intended target is less than twenty-five feet away. Let's look at some statistics:

**New York City Police Study on their own officers:** (http://pointshooting.com/)

*From Sept 1854 to Dec 1979, 254 Officers died from wounds received in an armed encounter. The shooting distance in 90% of those cases was less than 15 feet.*

*Contact to 3 feet ... 34%*

*3 feet to 6 feet ...... 47%*

*6 feet to 15 feet ..... 9%*

In 70% of the cases reviewed, sight alignment was not used. Officers reported that they used instinctive or point shooting. As the distance between the Officer and his opponent increased, some type of aiming was reported in 20% of the cases. This aiming or sighting ran from using the barrel as an aiming reference to picking up the front sight and utilizing fine sight alignment.

The remaining 10% could not remember whether they had aimed or pointed and fired the weapon instinctively.

The Police Officer's potential for hitting his adversary during armed confrontation has increased over the years and stands at slightly over 25% of the rounds fired. An assailant's skill was 11% in 1979.

In 1990 the overall Police hit potential was 19%. Where distances could be determined, the hit percentages at distances under 15 yards were:

Less than 3 yards ..... 38%

3 yards to 7 yards .. 11.5%

7 yards to 15 yards .. 9.4%

In 1992 the overall Police hit potential was 17%. Where distances could be determined, the hit percentages at distances under 15 yards were:

Less than 3 yards ..... 28%

3 yards to 7 yards .... 11%

7 yards to 15 yards . 4.2%

You could conclude from the New York City study that if you are going to be shot, it will be from only a few feet away. These are police statistics and I am not aware of any similar statistics for civilians. However, I believe police officers exercise caution whenever possible and you will probably be more likely to get closer to your shooter than they do.

You should also include that the likelihood of shooting back and hitting the target is slim. Keep in mind these were trained police officers who do this stuff for a living. You are not likely going to do as well as they did. You should also keep in mind that there will often be more than one police officer dispatched to these scenes and they usually have help bringing the situation to a resolution... help from other armed police officers equally trained. You probably won't have that luxury. But that is just one department. Now let's look at police officers across the country through statistics maintained and evaluated by the FBI.

Here are the FBI's 1988 - 1997 stats on Law Enforcement Officers Feloniously Killed with firearms depicting details on the distance between victim Officers and Offenders:

Total Officers killed ---- 633
Contact to 5 feet ------- 337 -- 53%
6 feet to 10 feet --------- 132 -- 21%
11 feet to 20 feet --------- 73 -- 12%
21 feet to 50 feet ----------53 --- 8%
Over 50 feet -------------- 38 --- 6%
86% were killed within 21 feet.

Here are the FBI's 1994 - 2003 stats on Law Enforcement Officers Feloniously Killed with firearms depicting details on the distance between victim officer and offenders.

Total Officers killed --- 568

Here are the FBI's 1994 - 2003 stats on Law Enforcement Officers Feloniously Killed with firearms depicting details on the distance between victim officer and offenders.

Total Officers killed --- 568
Contact to 5 feet ------- 286 --50%
6 feet to 10 feet -------- 122 -- 22%
11 feet to 20 feet -------- 60 -- 11%
21 feet to 50 feet -------- 47 --- 8%
Over 50 feet ------------- 43 --- 8%

Distance not reported 10 /83% were killed within 21 feet.

Aside from the fact most studies show that shootings occur in low light (darkness) situations, the likelihood of seeing your sights and aligning them on the target is slim, even with night sights.

*Here's what the US Army says about our instinctive pointing ability in its 2003 Field Manual 3-23.35: (from Point Shoot)*

*Combat Training with Pistols M9 AND M11.*
*"Everyone has the ability to point at an object."*

*"When a soldier points, he instinctively points at the feature on the object on which his eyes are focused. An impulse from the brain causes the arm and hand to stop when the finger reaches the proper position."*
*"When the eyes are shifted to a new object or feature, the finger, hand, and arm also shift to this point."*
*"It is this inherent trait that can be used by a soldier to rapidly and accurately engage targets."*

Think about this for a second. If you are standing out on the street and somebody asks you for directions nearby and you point in that direction, your eyes follow your hands (and vice-versa) and synchronize to focus precisely where you are pointing. If you use the barrel of a handgun as an extension of your pointer finger, the same thing will happen.

Before we totally leave the subject of statistics I would like to point out the crime in Jackson, Mississippi since this book is written for Mississippi residents primarily and Jackson happens to be the capitol city. Statistics are often a few years old because collection, analysis and distribution takes time after the fact. The 2011 statistics are not out yet and of course 2012 has not ended (at print time). Any of the crimes listed in the chart you are about to see, could have resulted in a gunfight. However, let's look at murder only for now, and focus on 2008. You can see there were 63 murders in Jackson during that year. However, there were only 41 police officers killed in the entire United States and its possessions.

*The police officer deaths occurred in 19 states. The number of officers feloniously killed in 2008 decreased by 17 compared with the 2007 figure (58 officers). The 5 and 10 year comparisons also showed decreases in the number of felonious deaths, down 16 from the 2004 number (57 officers) and a decrease of 1 from the 1999 total (42 officers). FBI Report.*

Of course to be statistically correct you would need to compare the number of citizens in Jackson to the number of police officers in the country to get an accurate reading. But the fact that 63 citizens were killed on the streets of Jackson, while only 41 police officers were killed responding to all the crimes you see below, tells me I would be less likely to die as a police officer anywhere in the US than as a citizen just trying to get by in Jackson, Mississippi. Does that make you want to arm yourself if you live in Jackson?

Here are the Jackson Police statistics for inside the city only:

| Crime in Jackson by Year | | | | | | | | | | | |
|---|---|---|---|---|---|---|---|---|---|---|---|
| ‡ Type | ▾ 1999 | ‡ 2001 | ‡ 2002 | ‡ 2003 | ‡ 2004 | ‡ 2005 | ‡ 2006 | ‡ 2007 | ‡ 2008 | ‡ 2009 | ‡ 2010 |
| Murders (per 100,000) | 45 (23.7) | 50 (27.0) | 49 (26.3) | 45 (24.8) | 53 (29.3) | 38 (21.1) | 40 (22.6) | 46 (26.2) | 63 (36.1) | 37 (21.4) | 41 (23.5) |
| Rapes (per 100,000) | 248 (130.6) | 218 (117.8) | 182 (97.8) | 179 (98.6) | 165 (91.2) | 158 (87.6) | 160 (90.2) | 141 (80.3) | 136 (77.8) | 124 (71.8) | 101 (58.0) |
| Robberies (per 100,000) | 1,096 (577.1) | 1,044 (564.0) | 1,074 (577.4) | 962 (530.1) | 678 (374.7) | 612 (339.2) | 1,022 (576.3) | 862 (491.1) | 942 (539.1) | 958 (554.4) | 1,086 (623.6) |
| Assaults (per 100,000) | 691 (363.8) | 654 (353.3) | 497 (267.2) | 462 (254.6) | 376 (207.8) | 417 (231.1) | 514 (289.8) | 463 (263.8) | 511 (292.4) | 396 (229.2) | 490 (281.4) |
| Burglaries (per 100,000) | 4,814 (2,534.6) | 4,683 (2,529.7) | 4,377 (2,353.1) | 4,369 (2,407.4) | 3,400 (1,879.0) | 3,139 (1,739.9) | 3,817 (2,152.4) | 3,897 (2,220.2) | 4,334 (2,480.3) | 4,569 (2,644.1) | 4,818 (2,766.5) |
| Thefts (per 100,000) | 9,703 (5,108.7) | 8,972 (4,846.5) | 8,669 (4,660.5) | 8,323 (4,586.2) | 6,846 (3,783.3) | 6,960 (3,857.7) | 7,534 (4,248.5) | 6,984 (3,978.9) | 6,990 (4,000.4) | 6,994 (4,047.5) | 6,877 (3,948.8) |
| Auto thefts (per 100,000) | 3,475 (1,829.6) | 2,965 (1,601.6) | 2,800 (1,505.3) | 2,804 (1,545.1) | 2,024 (1,118.5) | 1,909 (1,058.1) | 1,857 (1,047.2) | 1,584 (902.4) | 1,711 (979.2) | 1,619 (936.9) | 1,555 (892.9) |
| Arson (per 100,000) | 32 (16.8) | 96 (51.9) | 73 (39.2) | 59 (32.5) | 52 (28.7) | 59 (32.7) | 65 (36.7) | 39 (22.2) | 81 (46.4) | 113 (65.4) | 83 (47.7) |
| City-data.com crime index (higher means more crime, U.S. average = 309.9) | 901.2 | 863.5 | 807.1 | 792.4 | 640.3 | 604.4 | 732.5 | 684.8 | 746.2 | 714.8 | 739.7 |

**Source: Jackson PD website**

In early 1993, I purchased an electronic firearms simulator. It was able to measure two things, speed and accuracy. Judgment was a third factor but the machine had no way of measuring that by itself. However, you could film a scene consistent with your use of force laws and get a pretty good idea as to whether or not the shooter acted in accordance with those laws. That was not always true. In fact, the real issue was how well the shooter could defend his or her actions. Depending on the amount of pre-engagement information the shooter was given, and whether or not the action he saw would have placed him in fear of his life if the scenario had been real, "shoot or not shooting" could sometimes be argued either way.

I learned other things from the use of the system though. On many occasions, the police officers being trained fired, not center mass, where he or she had been trained, rather they hit the gun, or a shot was recorded on the plane of the gun. In many of those cases, the gun was down at the side of the assailant in a hip-shooting situation. The shot striking the suspect firearm was in most cases ten to fifteen inches away from upper torso center mass. Many of the police officer students claimed they were "shooting the gun out of the suspect's hand." I am not going to tell you that a police officer would lie about a thing like that, but I will tell you they had no training to do so, and should have been firing at dead center mass (sometimes head shots, with SWAT team members depending on the department).

What I also learned was that most of the scenarios where the officer shot at, or around the gun, it was a very fast scene, not giving the officer time to aim. So why did so many shoot at or around the weapon? My findings were for two reasons. One was that our eyes focus on a threat and the other is that we often develop "tunnel vision." These officers focused on the threat and fired at the threat. All the center mass training in the world had not trained that out of them. Other scenes that were slow with plenty of time to aim and the suspects telegraphed their movements, led to shots in center mass.

As a private citizen, if involved in a fire-fight, you will likely be in a close-in shoot situation, I am going to suggest you try to use the sights, but have you shoot without them so you can choose the method that works best for you, armed with this information. Whichever technique you choose, I encourage you to practice, practice, and practice some more. If you live in the country where you can shoot any time, set up a chair to simulate a car seat and shoot to your left as if defending yourself against a carjacker if you choose to shoot in that situation. Practice one handed, left handed, both hands, with the weapon at your side, slightly in front of your torso, arms extended, and any other way you can think of that could best simulate all possible scenarios.

Your assailant may only be two feet away, and you may not be able to extend your arms, assume a certain stance, or breath as if you were on the firing range. Your grip may only be with one hand, or your hands may be shaking so badly, you can't control the weapon. You will have to do the best you can with the circumstances you are in. The more different ways you practice, the better prepared you will be.

Don't get hung up on stance, because to tell you the truth, you should be moving while shooting, and that too, will prevent you from aiming in most cases unless you are a highly trained, much practiced combat marksman. Moving targets are harder to hit. Don't make yourself an easy one.

Going back briefly to the simulator, many police officers will gripe, or make light of a system that doesn't give you all the realism available in real life. Well first of all, you will never get ALL the realism, unless you are using live rounds with your opponent trying to kill you and you him. I have heard complaints about simulator handguns not having the right, or any recoil. I have heard that the shots are not loud enough to be realistic.

Many studies where police officers were interviewed in post shooting scenarios, said they never felt the recoil; the shots sounded like "pops;" they couldn't remember using the sights; time was distorted into slow motion, they had tunnel vision, and could only see the suspect and/or his gun.

My question to those people would be, "When you get out of your patrol car and approach a suspect, do you have Mickey Mouse ears on? Do you have shooting glasses on? Is there somebody standing over your shoulder telling you when to fire and/or cease fire? Those are range problems that keep you from having realism. Simulators will have their own.

I personally don't care if the simulator gun makes a noise at all. Nor do I care if it has recoil. I don't even care if it is the same kind of gun I carry or not. You know why? Because the simulator is not made to teach you the feel of a weapon, recoil of a shot fired, or the sound of a gunshot. It was developed to help teach you when to use good judgment and be able to defend the judgment you used. It was designed to show you how fast you reacted to a threat and what, if any area of the body you struck your suspect with returned fire. Maybe you missed; maybe you wounded the suspect; or maybe you hit a kill zone.

The first simulator I was exposed to when I was in the police academy in 1976 didn't even use guns. It was a television video narrated by actor Peter Faulk (Columbo). We were shown scenes and given some pre-scene information and then the video was paused by our instructor. We had to write down, or tell the instructor what our actions entailed. After that, the video was started back, and you saw the rest of the scene, to determine whether or not your actions were in accordance with the law and/or whether or not you could justify your actions. I loved it.

I will attempt to do the same thing in this book with very limited scenarios where you will be shown a picture and given some information. You may want to sit down with your lawyer and ask him/her if you chose a particular action, if he or she could defend you on those actions. I can't, and won't advise you, although I might throw in my two cents, and tell you what I might have done under the same or similar circumstance.

I see my job as teaching you how to recognize certain weapons, how to become a novice at identifying parts of those weapons, safe handling of them and shooting them proficiently enough to achieve only MINIMUM qualification scores. I feel the need to expose you to statistics and tactics to the point that you will think about what you will do, and how you will do it.

I can provide you the laws, but it is up to you to interpret them or get advice from an attorney. I can provide you scenarios, but I won't be the guy representing you when you go to court to defend your actions. Don't wait until it happens before getting advice from an attorney.

You need to learn how to shoot on your own, while lying on your back, lying on your stomach, sitting, kneeling, prone, on both knees, lying on your side, and any other predicament you think you might find yourself in. You also need to learn on your own how to shoot frontwards, sideways, around corners, under cars, from up high, from down low, while running and any other way you can think of. Why? Because those are the situations you are most likely to find yourself in. It won't be standing in a Weaver stance (covered later), with a stationary target directly in front of you, and unlike that target, your adversary WILL be a threat to you.

Lastly, I want you to realize that only slightly missing the target to the left or right, at close range could have a devastating affect on your accuracy or shot placement. As you increase your distance from the target by moving back, your angle of error will decrease your accuracy.

In the next illustration, I will attempt to explain what happens. Even if you remain positioned exactly in front of the center of the target, as you move back from (in this case) five to fifteen feet, the angle stays the same, but the distance moves your shot placement further and further from the center line. This is one argument for using your sights. However, the fact that most shootings take place within this number of feet, and the fact that you will most likely hit somewhere near center mass at this distance without aiming, is an argument for the point-shoot technique. Again, it is all about practice.

NOTE:

This type error could be caused by improper aim point, but more often at this distance, it is pulling the gun to the right with your trigger pull rather than straight back.

Shooting Lanes

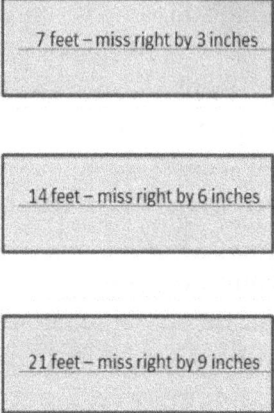

7 feet – miss right by 3 inches

14 feet – miss right by 6 inches

21 feet – miss right by 9 inches

If you are positioned 7 feet from the target and miss the X center ring by 3 inches, you will miss by 6 inches when you double the distance to 14 feet, and your miss will be tripled to 9 inches when you move back to a 21 foot shot (without correction).

Remember, most police officers are killed in less than 21 feet, so that is the range you need to concentrate on.

The hit rate at 21 feet is about 25 percent for trained police officers, so you only have at best a 1 out of 4 chance at hitting your target with your first shot. However, that chance rises as you get closer to the target.

Bullet Trace Lines

By the way, a handgun shoots one round at a time and only places additional rounds to one side or the other (or up and down) as you move the barrel with succeeding shots. However, a shotgun spreads out many rounds at one time on a target, and the pattern gets bigger (just like the spread of individual rounds on the illustration above) as the distance increases. But this will give you an idea what a shotgun will do up close to a human body:

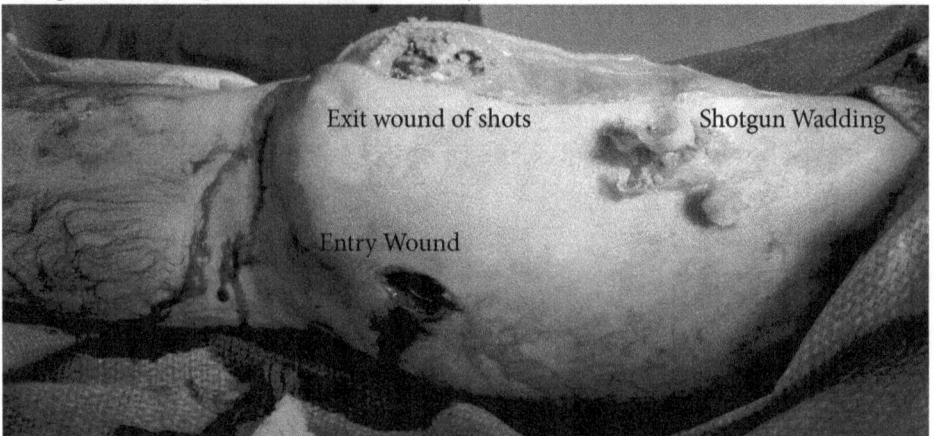

Exit wound of shots

Shotgun Wadding

Entry Wound

# CHAPTER FIVE

## Judgmental Considerations/Choices

This portion of the book deals with questioning your knowledge and reasoning for using a weapon in your defense, or the defense of another. Please look at the scenario, read the information you are given and decide what you would do. Grab a pad of paper and jot down your responses as to what you would do, why you would do it, and defend your actions based on your interpretations of the law and the threat at hand. **These scenes and your responses ARE NOT instructive in nature, rather a means to stimulate thought and have you realize that using a weapon carries with it, a great degree of responsibility, sometimes determining if someone will live or die.** It also means you must be able to defend your decisions and be prepared to face the consequences. Those consequences could be lifetime nightmares, life in prison, death sentence, huge lawyer fees and possible judgments that could be in the millions of dollars. However, failure to act could also result in many of these, as well as the loss of your own life, or someone you are trying to protect. It is not easy, or enjoyable, but a necessary evil. Good Luck!

**Scenario 1:**

As a private citizen licensed to carry a concealed weapon and carrying it at the time, would you shoot this armed person if you were within 25 feet?

## Comments:

Taking a shot in this situation would be extremely dangerous for the lady, as well as the child. You would have to be able to draw extremely fast and render a precision shot without hitting the innocent people. Most of us are not that proficient with a firearm and even for those who are, it would be a last resort when all else has failed.

One might consider calling 911. A seasoned hostage negotiator might be able to get to the bottom of what ever this person wants and bring this situation to a successful conclusion. Buying time would probably be helpful.

## Observations:

The suspect has left his entire left side exposed, to include his center mass. The weapon he is using is a double action pistol which would require squeezing the entire trigger pull rather than just touching it, as would be the case if the hammer were back. These observations are important intelligence for a SWAT team, or person capable of extreme accuracy in shot placement should all else fail. As long as the suspect remains where he is, and doesn't attempt to become mobile, the situation might be easier to bring under control. Many situations like this one are of a domestic nature and involve child custody. They are extremely dangerous because often people without even a record of traffic offenses commit murder as a "crime of passion." They don't think about the consequences of their actions and they resist reasoning.

## Monday Morning Quarterback:

In that capacity, what I might have done is try to draw my weapon to place him under a similar threat, while at the same time, hitting my number one key pre-programmed on my cell phone to summons the police in an attempt to contain the situation. That is not to say that I would have been successful though. You might have chosen a very different action and may well be able to defend it, even better than I can. If other facts had entered the scenario, there might have been a very different outcome. This is just an exercise to stimulate your thoughts and reasoning.

**Scenario 2:**

You are driving down the road in your car and hear on your police scanner that a man dressed in a dark business suit has robbed the local bank and was last seen running through wooded lots adjacent to the bank. This picture is what you see just as you pass one of those wooded lots. What actions would you take if any? Would you shoot? Would you call the police on your cell phone and keep driving? Would you pull over and try to keep him under surveillance. Would you stop and call out the window at him, telling him to give up? Why would you do, or not do whatever you have chosen? Please defend your actions on a piece of paper.

**Comments:**

Remember from the call on the scanner, there was a bank robber last seen running into the nearby wooded lots. Let's assume for a moment that the man in the picture is that man. He has indeed committed a felony, but is he armed? Did he rob the bank using only a note? Does he pose a danger to me? Can I keep driving. Do I have a responsibility to stop and try to take some action? Am I sure this is the right man? Could this be a real estate agent posting a "For Sale" sign, who just saw a snake?

**Observations:**

We know from the scanner that the police are aware of the situation. The man described on the scanner was wearing a dark business suit and this man is wearing a light business suit. There was no mention of a hat or brief case in the call. This man is not displaying any sign of a weapon, but then again, they never said he did at the bank either. He could be the robber, but then again, he may not be. He doesn't appear to be any threat to potential hostages since he is entering the woods, possibly trying to escape.

**Monday Morning Quarterback:**

Even though he is in a light business suit and the report on the scanner indicated the robber was dressed in a dark suit, it is not uncommon at all for witnesses to reveal incorrect information, or forget information, especially under frightening situations. I wouldn't rule this man out as being the suspect. However, this man poses no immediate threat to me. I would probably turn my car around and call the police on my cell phone while doing my best to keep him under surveillance at a safe distance in case he is armed. I would be on the lookout for any accomplices he may have, or a nearby getaway car. Again, if he got into one, I would do my best to maintain surveillance at a safe distance while giving the police as much information as I could about the car and location. Pursuing him into the woods would be a dangerous move that I would leave to the police.

**Scenario 3:**

Suicide committed by our soldiers is at a higher rate than it has been in the history of our country. All of us would like to do anything we can to save the lives of our soldiers. The man in this picture may feel he has no will to live. Maybe his wife left him while he was on the battlefield, or his baby died before he ever got a chance to see him or her. Because of other obstructions in the room, this picture is all you see at the present time. Do you feel he poses a threat to you? Do you feel an obligation to intervene? What action, (if any) would you take. Please defend your responses.

Record your responses before looking at the next page. What would you do? Why? What is likely to be the outcome?

**Comments:**

While we all feel a duty to do something, we must take into consideration the state of mind this young man might be in. If he feels the need to take his own life, taking somebody else's life who might be seen as an obstruction to him might be of no consequence to him. If he wants to die that badly and you attempt to interfere, he may take you out first. Although you may see this as a scene to run up and plead, it might be wise to a least have your weapon drawn just in case.

**Observations:**

He is dressed as a soldier. That tells me he probably is, or probably was a soldier. That also means he is probably proficient in the use of firearms and not to be reckoned with. He had the pistol in his mouth and seemed to be determined to take his own life. You can't see his other hand in this scene or anything else for that matter. He may have already taken the lives of other family members. Again, killing you may be of no consequence to him.

**Monday Morning Quarterback:**

If you decide to approach him, this may be the next scene you see:

**Scenario 4:**

You hear a noise in your house in the middle of the night. You grab your gun off the night stand, walk through the kitchen and flip on the light. This is what you see and you have no idea who this man is and he is barely over an arm's length from you. What would you do? Why? Would you attempt to disarm him, or give him a chance to give up? What would you say to him if anything?

Record your answers on a pad of paper before viewing the next page. Describe your actions and why you did what you did.

**Comments:**

This is an intruder in your house. You don't know him and should have every reason in the world to fear for you life. He has a weapon capable of causing you serious and grevious bodily harm, if not death.

**Observations:**

From the looks on his face, he is angry. He is not just reading the manufacturer's name on the blade. He has the knife drawn back in an offensive manner and appears to be moving in your direction. Some people may say you should tell him to drop it, before shooting, if that is what you intend to do. Others may not. I would probably be thinking if this guy is so irrational that he would break into my house in the middle of the night and pick up a knife, then come at me in an attack mode, he is not likely to be rational enough to drop it if I tell him to. Therefore, I would be wasting valuable time in shouting at him. I could try and run, but he may attack me from behind.

**Monday Morning Quarterback:**

So far we have focused on guns as threats to us. This is our first scenario to consider knives, sometimes referred to as "edged weapons." Remember that a .38 caliber gun will make about a .38 caliber entry wound in most cases. A knife, on the other hand, can make any size injury the attacker wants and a knife never runs out of bullets. I would have shot the guy if possible.

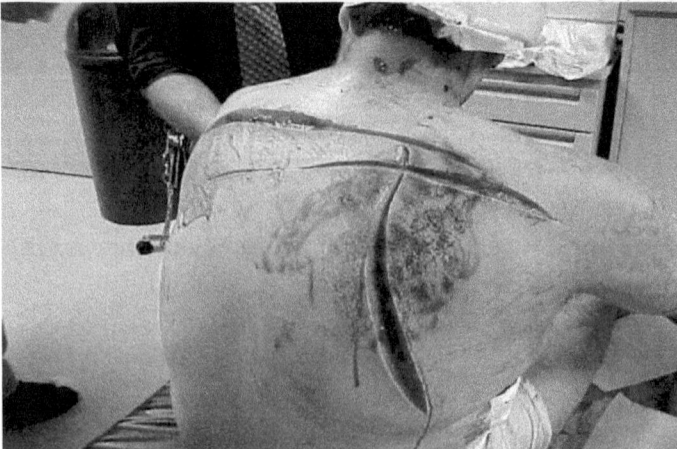

**Scenario 5:**

You are walking through a neighborhood looking at houses that have been foreclosed on, in hopes of getting a good deal. You walk down the side of one and suddenly, without warning, this is what you see at the rear corner of the house within a few feet of you. What action, if any do you take?

**Comments:**

This man clearly has the means and opportunity to cause you harm, if not death. He is within close proximity and already has the "weapon" drawn. If you shoot, you may be wrong. If you don't, you may be dead. Could you, or should you, attempt evasive action, like maybe running? Does it look like he is going to throw this brick at you, or use it as a blunt force trauma weapon to bash in your head? If you decide to shoot, can you draw and shoot fast enough to beat this guy at his game? If not, what if he knocks you down and takes advantage of your injuries, before taking your own weapon and uses it on you?

**Observations:**

Many people have lost their homes in the financial crisis we have faced. Many were forced out against their will. Many have torn out toilets, sinks, cabinets and other items just to make a statement to their mortgage companies. Some people don't like opportunists who show up for a good deal because of their bad luck. Some come close to losing their minds, or at least their ability to use good judgment in times like these. This man appears to have a crazed look on his face and could be dangerous. He has startled you and very likely put you in fear of your life.

**Monday Morning Quarterback:**

Depending on what was behind me, or to the side of me, I may have tired to flee, if only enough to create distance between the two of us while I got out my gun. If there was a fence, or something else to the side, I may try to take cover. I don't think I could have outdrawn, or shot him before he could have bashed in my head, if I remained at the same distance. However, if you fail to do something in a scenario like this, you may well lose your life. Nobody can tell you what is right based on the small amount of information we have. You would have to be in an omniscient position to give advice.

**Scenario 6:**

You are driving in town in the right hand lane. There is a car stopped at the red light in front of you. As you approach the rear of that car, someone bumps into you from behind. You start to turn around, or get out and another person jumps out of the passenger side of their car to your left, gun in hand. He tells you to put your hands up and get out of the car. You are stunned because you think you were involved in a simple rear end minor collision, but you quickly learn the people in the two cars are working in conjunction with each other to car-jack you. What do you do? Explain your actions.

**Comments:**

Here you sit in a boxed-in situation with little opportunity to do anything. From the looks on your face, you are amazed that this is even happening. As you contemplate what to do, you may decide to floorboard it and take your chances, but you look up and notice the light is now green, but the car in front of you has not moved. Could it also be involved in this attack?

**Observations:**

This crime is clearly a felony. The perpetrator is committing a robbery. He is attempting to take your property against your will by placing you in fear of your life. You should be in fear of your life at this point as you look down the barrel of his gun. He has forced you to put your hands in the air so you can't reach for your gun. Hopefully your gun wasn't on, or between the seats and now knocked onto the floorboard.

**Monday Morning Quarterback:**

The car is not worth your life. I don't think anyone would question your justification to shoot, but with the odds stacked against you, it would be unlikely that you would survive if you tried. Even if you have practiced quick-draw to the point that you are a master, trying to take any action puts you in grave danger. First you have a robber with a gun in your face at the window. He was apparently the passenger from the car on your left. That driver and/or additional passengers might be armed as well. Then you have the accomplice in the car behind that struck you. He and/or any passengers he has, might also be armed. Now you know the car in front is probably a part of this scam too, keeping you from speeding away. Any wrong move on your part could result in you receiving multiple gunshots. I won't say that you couldn't get out of this situation, but I will say that if you did, everything would have to be in your favor, and you would have to be a very lucky and blessed man. I would wave goodbye to the car, and call the police with all the information about the suspects, their vehicles and direction of travel that I could. I might look for a restroom, possibly a laundry, then I would call my insurance company.

**Scenario 7:**

You are on a crowded street and see a commotion in front of you. You walk past an alley and look to your side. This is what you see, some twenty feet in front of you. You might assume that a purse snatching has taken place and this guy must be the culprit. What do you do?

## Comments:

We don't know for sure what happened. If this purse had been unattended somewhere without the owner immediately present and in control, the crime might have been a simple theft. The value of the purse and its contents would have to be known to determine if it were a felony or a misdemeanor. If the value was under $500 under Mississippi law, it would be a misdemeanor and deadly force is probably not authorized under that condition. However, the purse may have been taken from a parked car that could have justified auto burglary, that could make it a felony. Then again, what about the fear of your life? What else is present that makes that a reality? There is a lot of uncertainty here, so what would you do and why?

## Observations:

The man has a stocking over his head. He has gloves on. He wants to conceal his identify at all cost, and may become violent in doing so. The fact that he has ducked into an alley and begun a search of the purse, probably means his is looking for valuables with plans of ditching the purse in the alley, or in a garbage can, not wanting to be caught with the identification in it. He won't be here long.

## Monday Morning Quarterback:

You are twenty feet or so away from him and he can't lunge far enough to cut you. Unless he is a proficient knife thrower (and few people are), at this distance he probably doesn't pose much of a threat to you. Although startled, it is not very likely that you are in fear of your life at this point, and you could run across the street to call the police. Almost everyone has a cell phone nowadays and I am assuming you have one. If not, you could start yelling for help like the English did in the old days of the "Hue and Cry" system. At the most, you may draw your gun on him, and attempt to keep him there until police arrive.

**Scenario 8:**

You have been in a downtown Jackson office building and parked your car in their garage. When you return to your car, this is what you see. What action, if any would you take and why?

**Comments:**

We don't know for sure what is happening here. It is pretty clear that this guy is breaking into your car, which would at least justify an attempted auto burglary.

**Observations:**

We can't tell if he is attempting to gain entry, so he can steal the car, or if he see's your wallet on the seat and that is what he wants. We don't know if the wallet has $10 in it or $800, so we don't know if the theft would constitute petty larceny, or grand larceny. No deadly force is authorized for petty larceny, but we can bank on the auto burglary as a felony and then determine if force should be escalated. From a safety point, there are at least two things that we should consider in this scenario from what we observe. One is, that it appears the cars are parked against the brick wall. If so, his only means of escape is to run past you. The other consideration is the fact that he has a sharp instrument in his hand, and could stab you with it as he passes by.

**Monday Morning Quarterback:**

He probably feels somewhat safe with the ski mask on, because if he gets away, you won't be able to identify him. He may even try to jump over the fenders of the car and run. He doesn't want to get caught, and will likely not confront you, especially if he sees you trying to draw a weapon. If he thinks he can beat you, he will go for it, and you will only see his shoe soles and elbows. If he does that, even though he has a potential weapon, he is fleeing and not putting you in fear of your life. Shooting a would-be car burglar in the back would be highly questionable. Shooting him in the chest before he has an attempt to run, would likely have to include justification of him drawing the sharp tool in an offensive stance towards you.

**Scenario 9:**

You hear what you think are gunshots near the back of your new property in town. You also hear what sounded like a woman screaming and you can't find your wife. You grab your gun and walk out back into the common area behind your house. You see this man and yell at him repeatedly to turn around. You get closer and yell louder and louder. There is no question in your mind that he can hear you, but he is refusing to comply. You aim your weapon at his back, and demand that he turn around with his hands up. At first he doesn't acknowledge you, but then with lightning speed, he spins around to the right, not raising both his hands but thrusting his right hand with something black in it towards you. What do you do and why?

**Comments:**

You are new to this neighborhood and don't know the people, or what goes on. However, you are not an idiot, and you know if you hear what you think may be gunshots followed by a woman screaming, there might be something wrong. Your suspicions are somewhat confirmed when you see a man out back moving away from you with his back to you and a bag under his arms that could contain a weapon. You are nervous because you can't see his right hand. To add icing to the cake, you yell at him, and he fails to respond. Finally you remove your weapon, point it at him, and demand that he put his hands up and turn around slowly as you move closer.

**Observations:**

What you see is what you get. You are having to rely on your senses to get to the bottom of this, because the suspect is not responding, or complying with your demands.

**Monday Morning Quarterback:**

Maybe the guy sensed at the last minute that you were there, or he saw you out his peripheral vision, and knew he better act quickly. Maybe this is a camera bag and he is going to take pictures.

Many of the previous scenarios could have changed drastically with only a few more details. It is impossible to calculate all the possible facts that could change, and in turn change the response necessary. You have only your feet to get you out of those situations, possibly your car, but the gun will get you deeper into the situation. Sometimes it may not be avoidable.

Nobody, except maybe a serial killer, wants to murder anybody. If you hear people bragging about people they have killed, (self-proclaimed war heros) they are probably either a murderer, or more likely a liar. That has been my experience anyway. Even soldiers who have had to do so, rarely, if ever brag about that. They may make a statement to that effect, or may respond to the question about it. However, if they make a point to brag about it, they are probably either lying, or need help. I would steer clear of them either way.

I would also like to address police officers in shoot situations. Our society has placed a great deal of scrutiny on their actions. Before you are quick to pass judgment on them, remember that dashboard cameras and witnesses just observe, and aren't facing the fear an officer may face when staring down a deadly situation. They have the luxury of re-wind and pause, taking all the time they want to make a decision. The officer has a fraction of a second with no second look. We have restricted the officer's actions and added to his toolbox. We require him to use other tools, before resorting to the handgun during an escalation of force.

An officer is given a baton, spray, handcuffs, taser and a handgun. In many of the situations you have seen in these scenarios, he would have had to start with one of those, and only escalated to a more serious one when the first one failed. Also, the suspect already knows what he is going to do and the officer has to see that action, recognize it as a threat, and his brain, working in conjunction with his eyes, must tell him to react. His reaction time after that, may, or may not save his life, and may, or may not take the suspect's life. If the officer ran, we would call him a coward. If he failed, we might call him a loser. If he prevailed we might call him a trigger-happy bully, or just say that he got lucky.

Impose the same scrutiny on yourself.

"*Many that live deserve death. And some die that deserve life. Can you give it to them? Then be not too eager to deal out death in the name of justice, fearing for your own safety. Even the wise cannot see all ends.*"

J.R.R. Tolkien

# CHAPTER SIX

## Range Safety/Equipment/Conduct

This chapter will take you from your home to the range. It will stress safety equipment you will need, and what to expect once you get to the range.

**FIREARMS SAFETY**

First and foremost, always consider a gun loaded until you know differently. Don't take anyone else's word for it. Check it yourself and do so in a safe manner. Make sure the muzzle is not pointed at, or near anyone. Never put your finger in the trigger guard until you are ready to fire. If the weapon is a revolver, point it down range, or away from any other person and open the cylinder to check for rounds. If it is a semi-automatic pistol, release the magazine, then pull back the slide with the muzzle pointed in a safe direction. Depending on what your intentions are, either empty it, or holster it.

**ENROUTE TO THE RANGE**

If you are going for training, your instructor may not want you to arrive armed even though you may already have a concealed weapon permit. Find out for sure before you leave. For the purpose of this book, let's assume he does not want you to arrive armed. We will start with the basics, and discuss what you should have with you, and how you should arrive.

**BAG**

When you pack for the range, you should have a small carry-bag like an athletic bag. It doesn't necessarily have to be designed for handguns, as long as it will carry what you need. It should have a hand-carry strap, and/or shoulder strap. A well-stocked bag would have the following:

## CONTENTS:

1.   Weapon
2.   Holster
3.   Belt
4.   Ammunition
5.   Ball cap
6.   Shatterproof Eye Protection
7.   Hearing Protection

**About $30 at Ebags.com**

    a.    Foam or rubber ear plugs
    b.    Muffs ("Mickey Mouse Ears")
8.   Hand Rag
9.   Bottled Water
10.  Waterless Hand Cleaner
11.  Small Note Pad
12.  Pen/Pencil
13.  Cell Phone
14.  Small first aid kit
15.  Small gun repair kit
16.  Chalk
17.  Gun Cleaning Kit

    a.    Bore Brush
    b.    Bore Swab
    c.    Cleaning pads
    d.    Solvent/Oil
    f.    Wiping rag

**Whole kit about $30 at Cabela's**

Not all of these items are necessary in all cases, but in some cases you may also need to bring a heavy duty stapler, staples, black and white "pasties," targets and a bucket, or other container for spent brass. Your instructor should tell you in advance what you will need to bring.

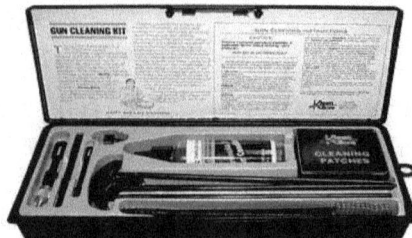

**$22 at Cabela's**

## ARRIVAL AT THE RANGE:

When you arrive at the range you may see something as simple as this. It may only be a few "lanes," or target positions. This is actually a pretty good range as far as safety is concerned. It has not only a berm in the back with trees behind it, but it has berms pushed up on each side too. It does not have asphalt or concrete walking lanes, or distance lanes, but it's not bad.

The Camp Dodge, IA Marine range below shows the distance lanes and the walkway lanes leading to the targets. It is well constructed, but it is not necessary to learn the best techniques.

**INDOOR RANGE:**

Ranges like this are hard to find. I know of only one in Jackson, on highway 80 near Clinton. It is the old Surplus Store. They are great for all-weather shooting. Most have motorized boxes like the one seen near the top of this picture in each line. The boxes house a motor that has a sprocket, or spool with a chain, or cable attached to move the targets downrange, or back to the shooter on an overhead rail system. Most have individual controls for the shooter to move the targets, although some are done by another person inside a control room. They have benches to rest weapons and other gear on. Large fans with filters and other devices withdraw dangerous gases from the building. The shooter never moves downrange on this type system. This particular range is at the Florida Gun Center located at: 1770 West 38th Place, Hialeah, FL 33012.

## WHO'S WHO AT THE RANGE:

Terminology varies, but for the most part, these are the terms you will hear. Don't be alarmed if the terms are inter-mingled:

**Rangemaster** - The guy overall in charge of the range. On small ranges, may share other titles, or assume additional responsibilities, rather than share them with extra help he doesn't have. Whether you call him the manager, owner, big-cheese, or whatever, he is the guy that will catch hell if something goes wrong. On large ranges, he may be in a tower with a bull horn, or public address system.

**Instructor** - May also be the rangemaster. This is the guy you listen to at all times. He will tell you what to do, when to do it, and how to, and how not to do it. You only do it after he tells you to, and even if you know the next step, you wait until he tells you. He will always be behind you, but maybe to the side when you are shooting. He will probably be, but not necessarily the same guy that gives you classroom instruction. He will use certain language that will be discussed shortly.

**Line Coach** - Sometimes known as a safety observer, but you may have both. Some ranges, or certifying agencies have safety rules that require a ratio of a certain amount of observers to the number of shooters. For example, you may have one instructor. However, you may have eight shooters on the line which may be hard to control. Therefore, an instructor may assign a safety observer, or coach for every four shooters. It could be for every two shooters. That may also depend on whether or not your shooters are first-time shooters, or experienced shooters.

**Shooter/Student** - The only person allowed on the lanes when shooting starts with the exception of the above individuals. No buddies, spectators, or other people will be allowed. Sometimes an instructor might allow a photographer, or remedial student-observer behind the line watching. But nobody ever moves forward of the firing line until the instructor is sure the line is clear, all weapons are holstered and he makes that decision by giving the order. Anybody else further back would only be known as spectators.

Some common language you may hear on the range from the instructor beind you is, "Ready on the Right...Ready on the Left?" If nobody raises their non-shooting hand, or does something stupid, the next command may be something like, "All ready on the firing line....Commence Fire." After the pre-determined number of shots have been fired without any mishaps, or mis-fires, the next command may be, "Cease Fire....holster your weapons." If the instructor wants to move you forward to look at your targets, next, he may say something like, "Is the line clear (or safe)?" If nobody says otherwise, he may say something like, "The line is clear (or safe)....move forward." You can then evaluate, and/or grade your target, then go back and start over, or leave the range, depending on the instructor's orders.

I decided to show this picture for several reasons. I can't tell for sure, but hope everybody is properly wearing hearing and eye protection. The instructor could be discussing issues without firing at this point. I suspect that is the case because they don't even have targets up yet.

However, this range at Lafayette Parish Sheriff's Office in Louisiana is well built. It is sometimes open to the public. Notice it has a lane directly in front of the targets paved in concrete, along with others at various distances. It has a large berm and concrete block walls separating the course from other areas. The width of the lanes is large enough for an instructor to stand behind the shooters without getting in their way, but close enough to observe detail.

I know this is a stretch, but the gentlemen in suspenders (let's call him Beaudreaux) could be a safety observer. He is ready for high water and I'll bet there are some crawfish pots boiling in the background somewhere. Don't badmouth my fine southern neighbors, even if they don't appear as you expected on such a professional range.

My Texas friends below are demonstrating what you will most likely see when you go to the range. The type of targets will vary depending on the instructor, and whether or not he uses those sanctioned by the organization that certified him as an instructor. It doesn't matter. What you want to be able to do is shoot somewhere around dead center mass.

Notice here that everybody is using just about the same stance. We will discuss that in more detail later, with emphasis on Isosceles and Weaver stances. This particular stance is a version of the Isosceles.

The American Rifleman model here demonstrates the use of the Weaver stance.

Notice that his feet are shoulder width apart, but not squared off on the target as they are in the above photo. He is turned sideways with his strong arm fully extended, and his weak arm slightly bent. He is looking down his arm as if to be shooting a rifle. Some variations of this include a one-hand technique, with the weak hand against the chest, or behind the shooter's back. There is also a kneeling variation of this stance.

In both Weaver and Isosceles, the shooter is presenting himself as a smaller target to his adversary. In Weaver, he turns slightly sideways, and in Isoceles, he his slightly crouched down.

## PHYSICAL ASPECTS:

I won't continue any discussions about stance other than what I have just shown. I say that because there is no telling what stance you may be in when you are forced to shoot your weapon. You could be in your car shooting sideways, in a chair shooting in front of you, in your bed shooting from lying on your back, or any other position, so I just encourage you to know what they are, and practice every potential scenario. I will now touch on other physical aspects of handling a weapon to include, trigger, grip, breathing, muscle memory and use of your eyes, all of which will be used in conjunction with the particular stance you choose.

**Trigger Finger** - Should always be outside the trigger guard until you are ready to pull the trigger.

**Trigger Strength** - Varies with each weapon, whether or not the trigger mechanism has been modified, and so on. The amount of strength it takes to pull the trigger is measured in foot pounds and is usually only known by the manufacturers, gunsmiths, armorers, or professional marksmen.

**Trigger Position** - The first joint of the finger should be on the trigger. Too much trigger finger, or not enough could result in rounds being pulled to one side or the other.

**Trigger Pull** - Should always be straight back, not pulling to one side. It should be pulled back steadily and in such a way that the shooter is surprised when the gun goes off. You should never pull it partially back and then snap quickly to intentionally cause the gun to go off. The pull should be gradual, and cause a complete surprise when you hear the bang.

**Trigger Release** - Allowing the trigger to reset as the next round moves into the chamber (semi-auto) and you recover the weapon from the recoil. On revolvers, the distance and feel will be the same for each shot. However, on semi-automatic pistols (most, especially those with hammers) the second, and subsequent pulls will be less, because the hammer will already be back from the slide, and your pull will not be bringing it back on the subsequent shots.

**Grip** - Will differ depending on whether or not you are using a revolver, or a semi-automatic (especially your weak hand). It could also depend on the size of your hand. However, the main point to make is that your strong hand (usually your right hand, unless you are left-handed) will wrap itself around the weapon after you have made a "V" using your thumb and forefinger with the remainder of your fingers falling inline under the index finger. Wrap your fingers around the weapon and support it with your weak hand.

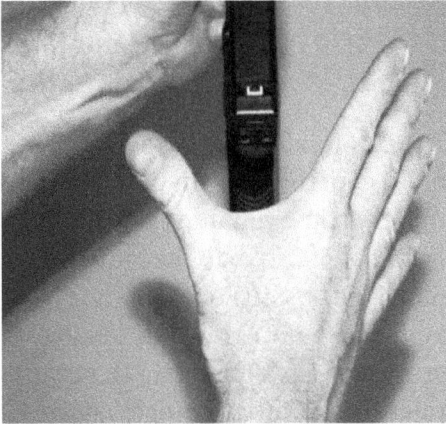

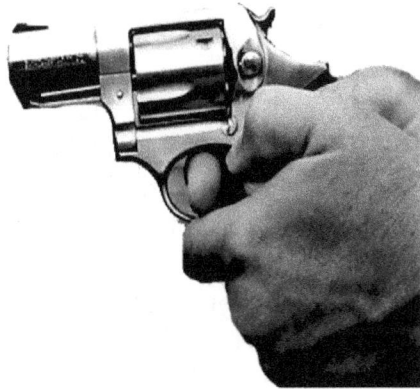

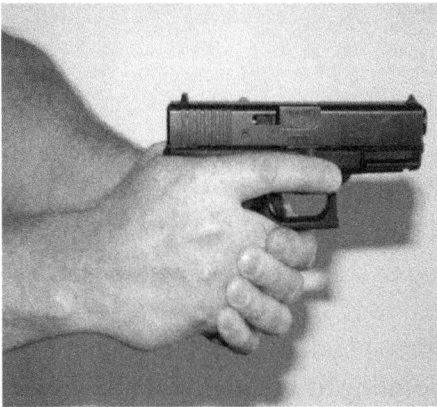

Notice finger outside trigger guard.   Left thumb <u>forward</u> on this photo, but most people prefer to have it either <u>up</u>, or <u>down.</u>

**BREATHING:**

If you are cool, calm and collected enough to take control of your involuntary bodily functions to the point that you can regulate your breathing, you probably are not in fear of your life. However, for instructive purposes, and to add that it is possible, if you have time to aim and wait on your suspect, I will point out what most other instructors will tell you. Take one deep breath and exhale. Take another deep breath and exhale. Lastly, just before squeezing the trigger, take another deep breath and let about half of it out, holding the rest. That should supply enough oxygen to your muscles for a few seconds to allow you to hold the gun steady enough to shoot.

**EYES:**

Some people will tell you to use your dominant eye. Others will tell you to keep both eyes open. I will tell you to experiment with both, and use which ever technique works best for you. Here's how you find out which eye is dominant. Find a spot, or decoration on the wall. Hold up the index finger of your strong hand until it is directly under the object. Focus on the object and your finger should be slightly out of focus. Now close your left eye. If your finger doesn't appear to move, your right eye is dominant. To be sure, now close your right eye. You will most likely see that your finger apears to have moved quiet a distance to your right.

**MUSCLE MEMORY:**

The best way I can describe muscle memory as it applies to you in this context, is to have you put both hands out in front of you with the index finger on your strong hand pointing outward as if it were the barrel of a gun. Now focus on an object, as if you were aiming to shoot at it. Now close your eyes, move your feet around slightly and wave your arms around. With your eyes still closed, try to point your finger where you remember the target being. Now open your eyes. If you are not pointing at the item, DO NOT move your arms or hands. Shift your body (feet) around slightly to compensate until you are back on target. Don't worry so much about the up and down sighting at this point. Now repeat that exercise several times until you can come back on target after opening your eyes, without arm movement.

## SIGHT PICTURE:

### Rear Sight

### Rear Sight alligned with Front Sight

## SUSPECT ARMED AND THREATENING YOU

The X is resting on top of the front sight; there are equal amounts of light on each side when looking through the rear side blade. The top of the front sight is oven with the top of the rear sight blade.

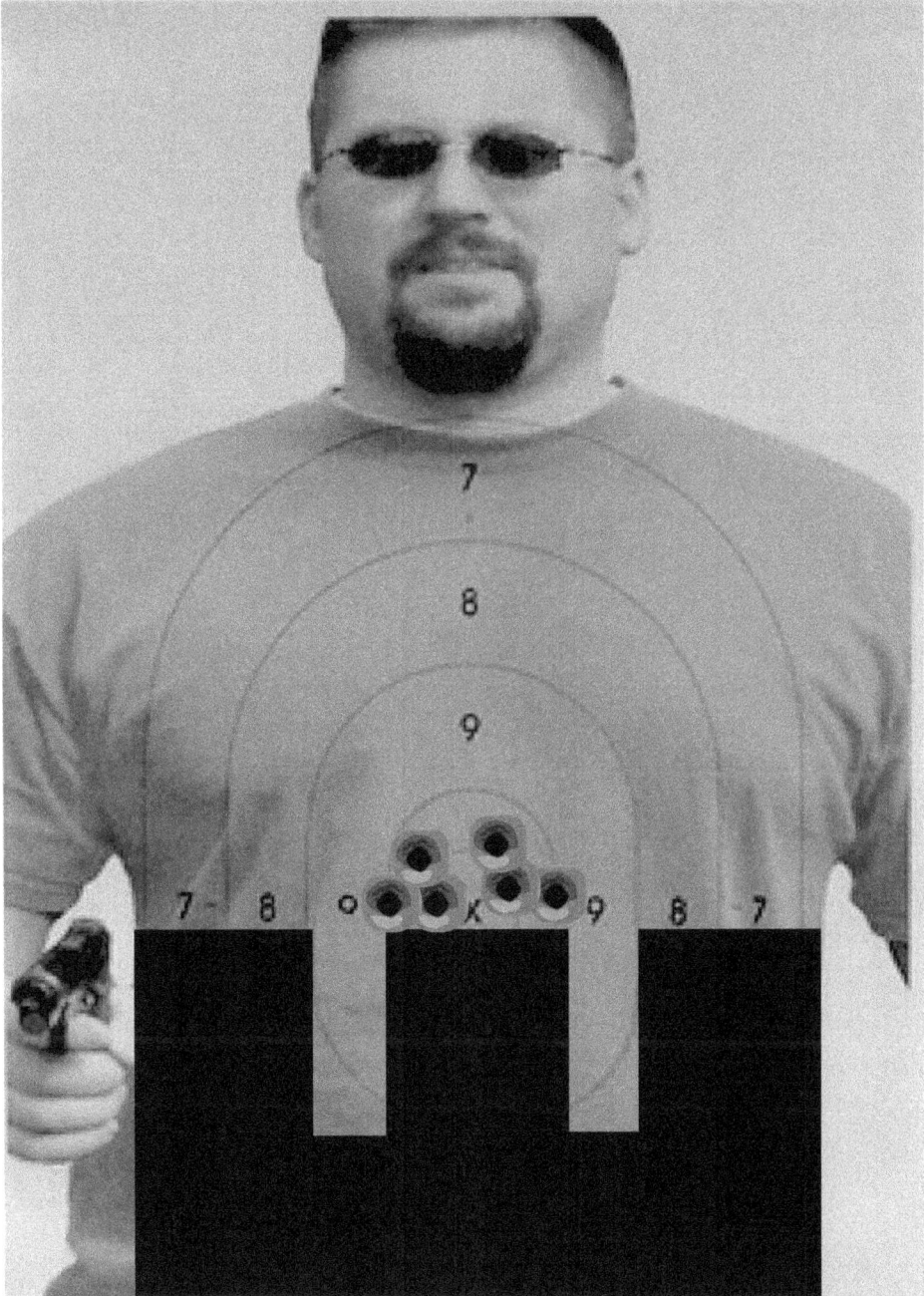

If you shot this target, you are just a lousy shot. There is no pattern and you are shooting all over the target. You need to go back and read/listen to everything you have been taught and try again.

If you shot this target, your shot placement is most likely off because your sights are really off, or you are aming to the right. This could also be a result of the amount of finger you have on the trigger or jerking the trigger.

The most likely cause of this pattern is simply that the muzzle is pointed to the left. The sights could be off since the group is so good.

The most likely cause of this pattern is the muzzle up too high, or the sights could be off since the group is so tight.

The most likely cause of this pattern is the muzzle being too low. It could be the sights off, but it also could be anticpating the shot, and jerking down on the trigger quickly. If your instructor would load your weapon without telling you he has only put two rounds in, when the gun clicks on the empty cylnder, the barrel going down would be very noticeable.

An instructor working with you can tell what problems you have. There could be all sorts of problems, most of which deal with all the things covered in this chapter. You must first know what the problems are, then correct them, then practice like you have never practiced before. Your instructor should be able to recommend drills to correct your problems.

Many of them may be correctable without having to use live fire. However, remember, no matter how good you are at shooting on the range, the game changes when you are in the public, scared to death, breathing heavily, seeing your family flash through your mind and hoping not to see a bright white light. Unfortunately, the first light you may see, might be the muzzle flash. The next one might be you, going to be with your maker.

I can't resist bringing up another story. We know how popular forensics shows are on TV now like CSI and others. The hype they generate is not that new though. I remember maybe thirty years ago reading a magazine and an old redneck sheriff from Texas (nothing wrong with rednecks or Texans though) sent a letter to the crime lab, that read something like this.

> *"I have heard all my life that the last thing a fellar saw just before he died was etched in his mind, or his eyeball or something. We had an ole boy that got shot right betwixt the eyes with a gov-ment 45. Why, hell, it popped both his eyes right out on his cheeks. One of 'em was flattened out, but we cut this other'n off at the stem and put it in this mayonaise jar for y'all to look at. Do you think y'all could check out this here eyeball and tell us what the last thang this ole boys saw was so we can solve this murder?"*

The toxicologists at the crime lab couldn't believe what they were reading. They carefully opened the box and sure enough, there was a big old eyeball floating in a mayonaise jar filled over half full with alcohol. It looked nasty to say the least. They thought at first about what they would say. They decided they didn't want to embarass the old sheriff, and they didn't want to piss him off either. They decided they owed him a response, so they went to work in their various lab rooms trying to come up with something the sheriff might understand. Their response was short, but gave the sheriff exactly what he asked for. It was the last thing old Rudy Earle saw before he died (next page).

Dear Sheriff:

As you requested, the last thing he saw (the .45 caliber bullet swirling towards his forehead) is shown below in this photograph.

No suspect, or anything else was visible to him in his last moments.

Sincerely,
Crime Lab Team

---

That is a funny situation, but there is nothing funny about murder. What most people don't realize, is that unlike what you see on TV, murder is not usually committed by Mafia bosses, or hit-men. Those responsible are usually friends, or family members, and the reason is usually the smallest and dumbest thing you could think of, sometimes only a few dollars.

The first murder I ever investigated was in Moss Point, Mississippi in 1975. I responded to the call based on a tip from the hospital ambulance crew who reported it as a suicide at about 5 a.m. When I got there, the crew had a gurney coming off the porch lifting it with the help of an elderly black man. Upon arrival, I assisted in getting a much younger black female (his wife, or live-in girlfriend) who had been shot in the head, up into the ambulance. After loading her, I turned to the old man and asked him why she would have killed herself. He quickly told me she had not killed herself, and that he had killed her because she had repeatedly refused to cook him three eggs for breakfast instead of two, noting that this morning would be the last.

I quickly pushed him up against the ambulance and handcuffed him. With alcohol still on his breath from the night before, and his shipyard badge clipped to his shirt, he offered no remorse. I told him if he ever got out, and re-married, I was certain that his new wife would fix him a dozen eggs and the chicken that laid them.

# CHAPTER SEVEN

## Nomenclature/Cleaning/Storage/Use

This chapter will help you identify and understand the workings of the average handgun. While you may not think that is important, there are many times when you will need to know what a particular part of the weapon is, how to clean it, and how that part may be disengaged for storage.

We will use the standard Smith and Wesson revolver user manuals, and move on to other models as the chapter progresses:

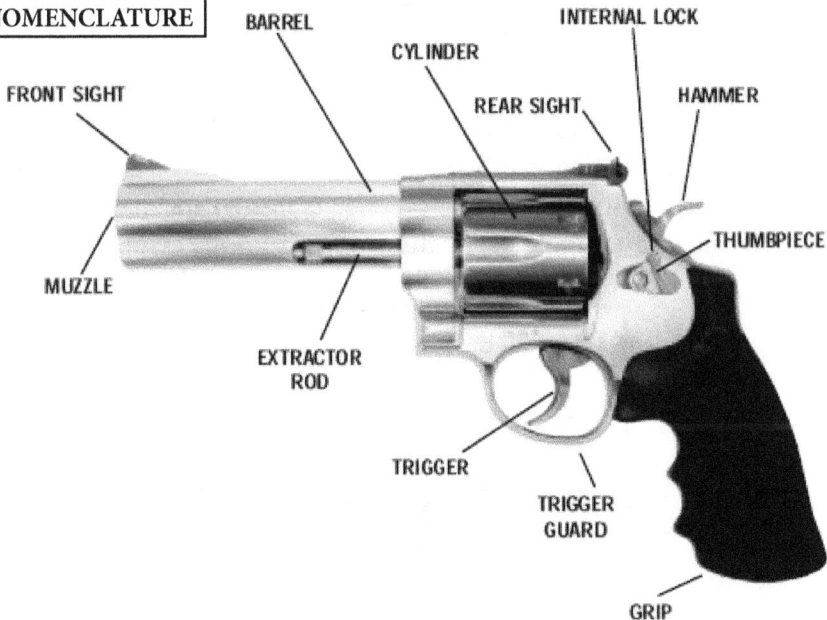

NOMENCLATURE

BARREL
CYLINDER
INTERNAL LOCK
FRONT SIGHT
REAR SIGHT
HAMMER
MUZZLE
THUMBPIECE
EXTRACTOR ROD
TRIGGER
TRIGGER GUARD
GRIP

**SMITH & WESSON**
**CUSTOMER SUPPORT CENTER**
**2100 ROOSEVELT AVENUE**
**SPRINGFIELD, MA 01104**
**TEL.: 1-800-331-0852**
**E-mail: qa@smith-wesson.com**

You may be handed a similar weapon by your instructor, or your own may be of similar design. He may ask you what the thumb piece is for. You may not know that answer. However, if you are familiar with the weapon at all, you will most likely know how to open the cylinder. That is precsely what the thumb piece, a spring loaded mechanism is used for.

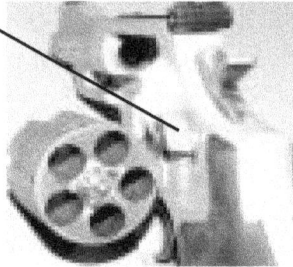

If you were asked to press the extractor rod a light bulb should go off inside your head telling you before you can do that, you must open the cylinder by using the thumb piece first. The extractor rod is also a spring loaded mechanism used to empty spent rounds from the cylinder.

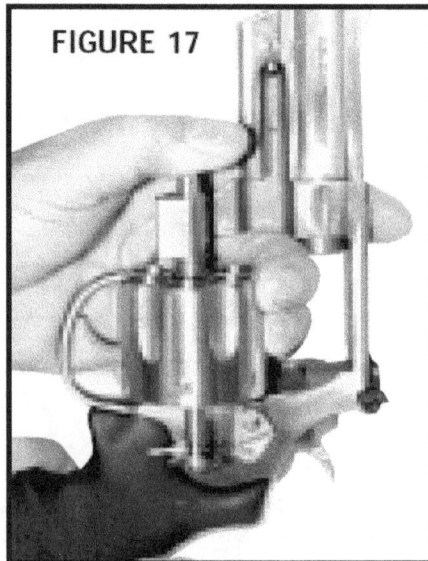

FIGURE 17

## AMMUNITION:

Ammo, as it is called for short, at least for the purposes of this lesson, describes any number of casings, usually, but not always made of brass, that contain a primer for ignition, powder for a propellant, and lead/steel (or combo) for a projectile. Some are round-nosed, some are hollow-point, some are armor-peircing. Below are two hollow-points followed by a cutaway version by Hornady:

Projectile

Casing

Powder (inside)

Primer

**LOADING:**

Much more information will be covered on these topics in your class room instruction, as well as on the range. These are very basic instructions from the firearms' manufacturer's materials.

To load your revolver, hold it in one hand with the muzzle pointed in a safe direction, away from you and others, while keeping your finger off the trigger and out of the trigger guard. Press the thumbpiece forward to unlock the cylinder. Push the cylinder to the left and place a round of the correct ammunition in each charge hole. Grasp the revolver in the shooting hand with your finger still outside the trigger guard, push the cylinder back into the frame until it locks into place.

**FIRING:**

There are two ways to fire your Smith & Wesson revolver. The first is in the double action mode, wherein the shooter fully pulls and holds the trigger to the rear, causing the hammer to fully cycle rearward and then release.

The second way to fire a revolver is in the single action mode, in which the hammer is first cocked and the trigger is then pulled and held to the rear.

A lesser amount of trigger pressure and motion are necessary to fire the revolver when the hammer is in the cocked position. As in any firing situation, continue to exercise great care in handling a revolver which has been placed in the single action or cocked mode.

**DE-COCKING:**

If you decide not to fire in single action from a cocked position, continue to point the firearm in a safe direction. De-cock the revolver as follows:

(1) Place the thumb of your free hand between the hammer and the frame of the handgun to prevent the hammer from moving fully forward until your finger is off the trigger and out of the trigger guard.

(2) Place the thumb of your firing hand on the hammer spur. You must always control the hammer with your thumbs when decocking the handgun. If the hammer slips while the trigger is held to the rear and you have failed to block the hammer travel, your handgun will fire.

(3) Apply pressure to the trigger to release the hammer. Immediately after the hammer has come out of cocked position, release the trigger and withdraw your finger from the trigger guard.

WARNING: *Failure to remove your finger from the trigger guard as soon as the hammer releases could cause the revolver to fire if your thumb slips off of the hammer spur.*

(4) Carefully ease the hammer forward while removing your other thumb from between the hammer and frame until the hammer is in the "at rest" position.

5) Practice this procedure with your unloaded revolver until you have mastered decocking. Always be aware of the hammer position. Never holster, carry or store a cocked revolver. Be sure the hammer is in the "at rest" position after de-cocking

# !! WARNING !!

**Ensure your firearm is unloaded before beginning to clean it. At all times follow the basic rules of safe gun handling.**

**CLEANING:**

After firing your handgun, be sure to unload it before performing any cleaning, or maintenance procedure. Your handgun should be cleaned by brushing the barrel bore and chamber (charge holes) with a good powder-removing solvent and bore brush. Wipe the areas clean with patches or a swab. Using a small brush dipped in solvent, remove all deposits from around the breech of the barrel, chamber (charge holes), extractor and adjacent areas which have been subjected to the action of powder or primer residue. Remove any residue on the frame with light brushing and a solvent. After cleaning the entire gun, use a cloth to apply a light film of high quality gun oil to all external metal surfaces and wipe clean.

### CAUTION:

You must follow the instructions provided with your gun cleaner and gun lubricant. Some cleaners can cause damage to your handguns.

### CAUTION:

You should avoid prolonged solvent immersion and prolonged ultrasonic cleaning of your firearm. Choice of solvent should be restricted to those products specifically developed for firearms maintenance. Instances of damage to a firearm's finish have been recorded when these cautions have been ignored. Ammoniated solvents or other strong alkaline solvents, should not be used on any Smith & Wesson firearm.

As a rule of thumb, if you would be comfortable applying the solvent of your choice to the finish of your automobile, it will probably be safe for use on your firearm. After the initial cleaning, there is usually some residue in both the barrel and cylinder that works out and becomes apparent within 24-48 hours. This can be removed with a bristle brush and a light re-application of powder removing solvent after which the oil film should be re-established on all surfaces.

Cleaning is considered essential in order to ensure the proper functioning of your handgun.

## STORING:

### DO NOT USE A LOCK ON A LOADED HANDGUN AND NEVER LOAD A LOCKED HANDGUN!!

Only you can determine what devices or practices are appropriate for the safe storage of your firearm and your ammunition.

### NEVER ASSUME THAT A "HIDING" PLACE IS A SECURE STORAGE METHOD.

Others may be aware of your storage location or come upon it by chance. It is your personal responsibility to use common sense when storing and securing your firearm and ammunition and to always make sure that it is not accessible to children or other unauthorized persons.

### FOLLOW THE LAW!!

You must be familiar with all local, state, and federal laws regarding the safe storage and transportation of your firearm. Failure to know and follow the law may result in unauthorized access or use of your firearm by another. Obey all laws relating to the storage and transportation of firearms.

### NEVER TRANSPORT A LOADED FIREARM.

When transporting your firearm, be sure it is unloaded and that the cylinder or action is open.

Now we will discuss the nomenclature of one of the more popular semi-automatic pistols manufactured by Sig Sauer. This information comes directly fromt their owners' manuals. Much of the information from the Smith and Wesson revolver section will apply. I will note differences as I see fit.

| | |
|---|---|
| 1 Frame | 21 Barrel |
| 2 Magazine Catch | 24 Slide |
| 5 Takedown Lever | 25 Front Sight |
| 8 Slide Catch Lever | 26 Rear Sight |
| 13 Trigger | 38 Magazine Floor Plate |
| 14 Hammer | 40 Decocking Lever |

Items numbered are the basic parts only. Other numbers not listed refer to parts needed by repair personnel. These are all you will need to know.

## DE-COCKING THE SEMI-AUTO:

**(Not all semi-automatic pistols have decocking mechanisms)**

The decocking lever on the SIG SAUER pistol is designed for the express purpose of decocking the firearm. The reason it is there is because it is not safe practice to decock a pistol by pulling the trigger and attempting to ease the hammer forward manually.
To decock your pistol, push down the decocking lever (keep your finger OFF the trigger while you do this).

---

## ⚠️ WARNING – DECOCKING LEVER

---

Always use the decocking lever to decock your SIG SAUER pistol. This is the only way to safely lower the hammer from the cocked position and prevent an accidental discharge. This warning applies to all pistols with decocking levers.

The positive way to safely lower the hammer is by use of the decocking lever. Never lower the hammer by pulling the trigger and attempting to ease the hammer forward manually. Manually lowering the hammer is dangerous and prevents full application of the pistol's safety features.

The decocking lever is the only proper means of lowering the hammer and assuring that the hammer rests in the intercept notch.

Again, DO NOT THUMB THE HAMMER DOWN:
the consequence can be serious injury or death – only and ALWAYS use the decocking lever!

**MAGAZINE FED:**

Unlike the revolver, semi-automatic weapons are fed by a magazine inserted into the grip.The number of rounds vary depending on the caliber or the weapon, the make and model. Some magazines are high-capacity for law enforcement use only depending on the state and when manufactured.

## 4.0 Handling

## 4.1 Preparation Instructions

If you have the pistol and ammunition, and have read and understood all of the safety instructions, you are now ready to use the pistol.

## 4.2 Loading the Magazine

1. Ensure the magazine is the proper type and caliber for the pistol.
2. Press down on the magazine follower with the cartridge case rim. Ensure the bullet is facing the front of the magazine.
3. Push the cartridge to the rear and under the magazine lips.
4. Repeat until the magazine holds the desired number of cartridges.

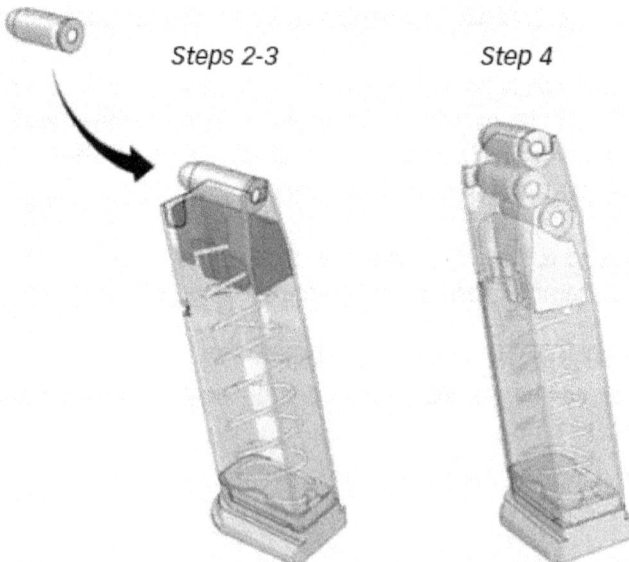

*Steps 2-3*                    *Step 4*

## 4.3 Loading the pistol (ready to fire)

1. Point the pistol in a safe direction.
2. Insert a full magazine and ensure it is engaged.
3. Pull the slide back fully and release, allowing the slide to fly forward.
4. Push down the decocking lever with your thumb (Not valid for DAO/DAK pistols).

---

### ⚠ WARNING – LOADED PISTOL

---

### THE PISTOL IS NOW LOADED AND READY TO FIRE.

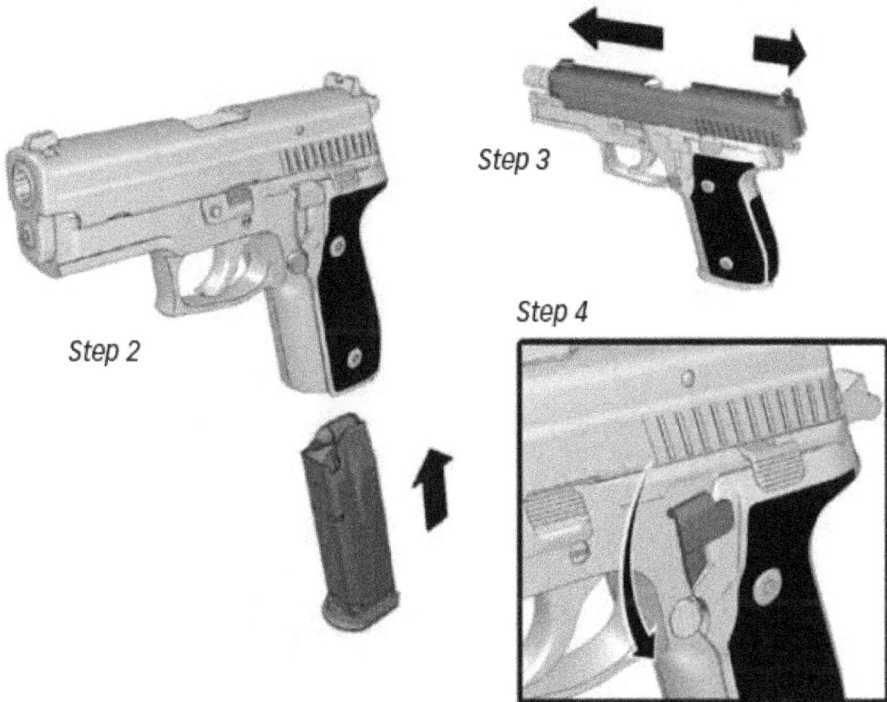

---

*Step 2*

*Step 3*

*Step 4*

The semi-automatic pistols must be broken down for cleaning. Below is an example:

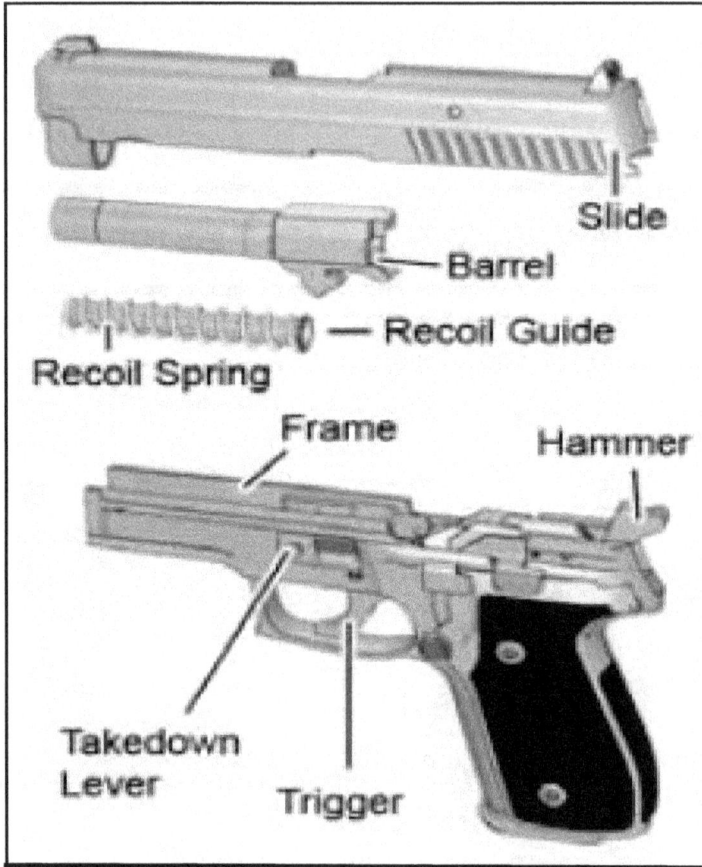

## AVOID OVER-LUBRICATING PARTS

For more information contact:

**SIG SAUER ACADEMY**

www.sigsaueracademy.com • (603) 679-2003

Main campus:              Epping, New Hampshire
Satellite Facilities:     Range 82, Midland, VA
                          NRA Whittington Center, Raton, NM

## SAFETY:

When transporting your firearm to and from shooting activities, keep it unloaded for your safety and for the safety of others. When storing your firearm, keep it separated from ammunition, under lock and key if possible, and out of the reach of children and other inexperienced or unauthorized persons.

---

## ⚠ WARNING – STORAGE

---

Never place or store any firearm in such a manner that it may be dislodged. Firearms should always be stored securely and unloaded, away from children and other unauthorized users. Use the locking device originally supplied with this firearm for storage. The use of a locking device or safety lock is only one aspect of responsible firearms storage. For increased safety, firearms should be stored unloaded and locked in a location that is both separate from their ammunition and inaccessible to children and any other unauthorized person.

## STORE SECURELY AND UNLOADED

---

## NEVER INSTALL THE LOCKING DEVICE INSIDE THE TRIGGER GUARD

**STORING IN LOCK BOXES:**

There are all types of lock boxes and safes for storing weapons. The lockboxes can be used in your car to transport the weapon and the safe can safely store your weapon(s) at your home. Both of these are available at Amazon.com. The lock box is about $120 and the safe is about $270.

**STORING (or carrying) ON YOUR PERSON:**

There are many types of holsters. Some clip on to the belt. Some have a loop on the inside that the belt feeds through. Some fit inside the pants with a clip on the outside. Some strap to your ankle, while others are carried in shoulder holsters. The prices vary from under twenty dollars, to over two hundred dollars. You should find what best works for you and what you can afford. These are made by different manufacturers, but are all available at: http://www.holsters4guns.com . Here are some examples:

Ankle Holster

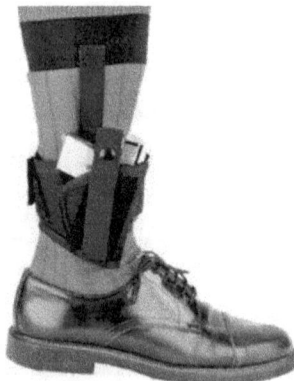

Hip Canvas with mag pouch        Inside Belt Canvas Holster

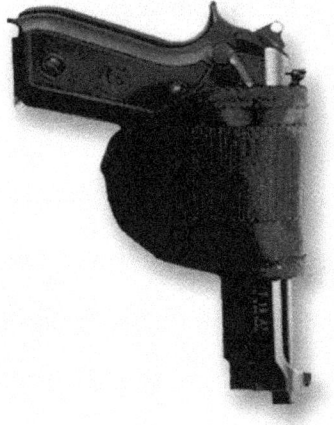

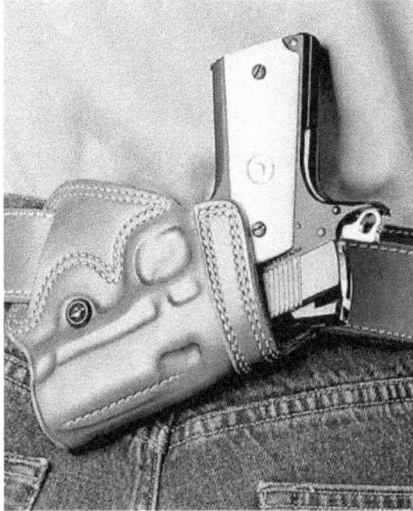

Small of the back leather holster (hammer back not recommended)

This is a fairly common type shoulder holster. The weapon rests vertically under the left shoulder, although some are amberdexitrious. The opposite side of the holster carries two magazines (speed loaders for revolvers). This particular one has fastners at the bottom on each side to hold it securely to your belt. Some variations include horizontal carries and some have additional pouches for handcuffs. Most are adjustable and have soft shoulder pads attached to the straps. I find them very comfortable and concealable.

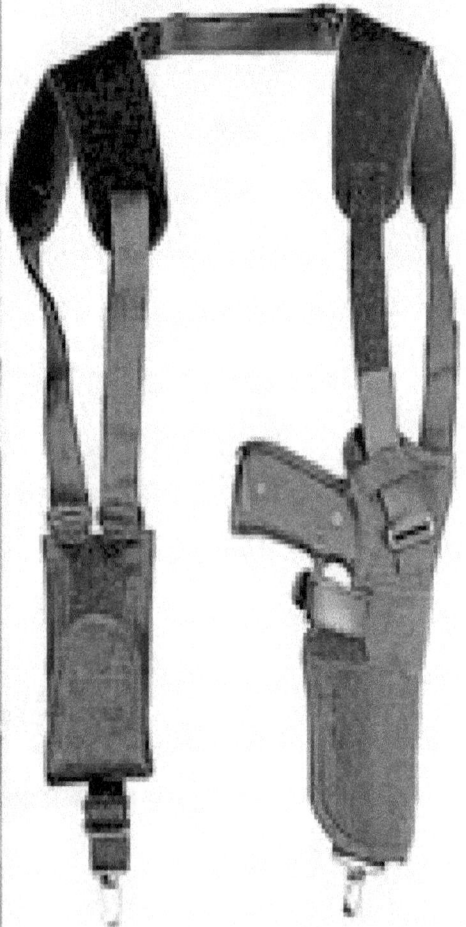

# CHAPTER EIGHT

## Reciprocity and Transporting

We have to realize that we are a mobile socieity. Some of us live near state lines with family and friends just a hop, skip and a a jump over that border. If we carry a gun, it becomes second nature to us and we may forget about it even being there when we make one of those trips.

Fortunately, other states have similar laws as ours regarding the carrying of concealed weapons. They too have an interest in traveling and being able to take their weapons with them.

I am not sure what the procedure was before, but there is a bill in our legislature as I type these lines, authorizing the Department of Public Safety to negotiate reciprocal agreements with their counterparts in other states for carrying concealed weapons. The legislation (House Bill 695) has been approved by the house and has been submitted to the senate (as of March 5, 2012). The revised wording from other similiar past bills reads:

> *The Department of Public Safety is authorized to enter into a reciprocal agreement with another state if that state requires a written agreement in order to recognize licenses to carry stun guns, concealed pistols or revolvers issued by this state.*

As it stands right now, we have reciprocal agreements with about half the states in the United States. There will always be those die-hard wiennies in certain northeastern states that detest handgun ownership. That has always amazed me since that's where the signer's of our constitution began.

Any time you plan to go into another state with your weapon strapped to your side, especially if you are going to get out of your car or spend the day or more there, you should go online and research their laws. It is not worth losing your weapon, your freedom, or the money in your pocket over. It doesn't take that much effort. Several sites online provide very detailed information. However, verify it with others because I have found some errors.

The information below came from http://www.usacarry.com/. While I don't attest to its accuracy, they seem to be current on laws as they change.

**Honors Mississippi Permit:**

Alabama, Alaska, Arizona, Arkansas, Georgia, Idaho, Indiana, Iowa, Kentucky, Louisiana, Minnesota, Mississippi, Missouri, Montana, North Carolina, Oklahoma, South Dakota, Tennessee, Texas, Utah, Vermont, Virginia, Washington, West Virginia, Wyoming

**Mississippi Permit Not Honored:**

California, Connecticut, Delaware, Hawaii, Kansas, Maine, Maryland, Massachusetts, Nebraska, Nevada, New Jersey, New Mexico, New York, North Dakota, Ohio, Oregon, Pennsylvania, Rhode Island, South Carolina, Wisconsin, Guam, Puerto Rico, Virgin Islands, Washington D.C. undefined

**Mississippi Res Permits Only:**

Colorado, Florida, Michigan, New Hampshire

**Right Denied:**

Illinois, American Samoa, N. Mariana Islands

**Below information is from this web site: http://www.ccrkba.org/**

Illinois (IL) is a "Non CCW state."

*Vermont (VT) , Alaska (AK) Arizona (AZ). Anyone who can legally own a firearm can carry it concealed. No Permit/license is required.

**Colorado (CO), Michigan (MI), South Carolina (SC), New Hampshire (NH), Florida (FL), Kansas (KS) and West Virginia (WV) only honor permits from residents of the issuing states.

These states issue Non-Resident Permits. Indiana (IN), Iowa (IA), Kentucky (KY), Maryland (MD), New Jersey (NJ), Oregon (OR) and Tennessee (TN) have very restrictive Non-Resident issue policies.

***TX only honors permits from DE issued by AG

You may think that knowledge of carrying concealed weapons into other states is a no-brainer. You may also think that our young well-trained ex-soldiers have enough common sense to know when, and where to carry concealed weapons. You may think bizarre cases of charging people with concealed weapons is old school. Take it a step further and you may think that the holder of a concealed weapon from another state, especially a businessman, would seriously question taking a concealed weapon into a New York City business. With all that in mind, I would like for you to read this excerpt from a January 16, 2012 FOX news article:

> *Ryan Jerome, a 28-year-old former private first class whose father and grandfather were Marines, faces three and a half years in prison after being arrested Sept. 27 for carrying a .45-caliber Ruger that was legally registered in his home state. Jerome, of West Bend, Ind., had approached security officers at the Empire State Building to check the weapon before he was taken into custody, according to his attorney, who said it was the man's first visit to New York City. Jerome had become a licensed precious metal jeweler in Indiana just prior to his trip to New York in September. His lawyer said Jerome drove to the state with his girlfriend to visit a Long Island-based refinery he was interested in possibly doing business with. He was carrying $15,000 worth of gold.*

Please, no dumb Marine jokes. This guy is in serious trouble. The City of New York doesn't take this kind of stuff lightly, no matter who you are.

Lets look at another New York case that was well-publicized after a professional athlete accidentally shot himself in the leg at a New York night club. This incident went beyond mere possession of a concealed weapon to actually discharging it, but he was charged with the possession only. It cost him two years of his life and all the money in the NFL couldn't get him out of it.

September 23, 2009

http://sports.espn.go.com/nfl/news/story?id=4493887

NEW YORK -- One-time Super Bowl hero Plaxico Burress was sentenced to two years in prison Tuesday for violating New York's stringent gun laws and was immediately taken into custody following his hearing.

Burress agreed to a plea deal last month and pleaded guilty to a lesser firearms charge. The charges stemmed from an incident late last fall, in which Burress accidentally shot himself in the thigh at a Manhattan nightclub with a gun that had not been licensed in New York.

Burress and team mate Antonio Pierce were at the Latin Quarter nightclub in Manhattan in late November 2008 when a gun that was tucked into Burress' waistband slipped down his leg and fired, shooting him in the right thigh.

The gun was not licensed in New York or in New Jersey, where Burress lived. His license to carry a concealed weapon in the state of Florida had expired in May 2008.

Burress, a nine-year veteran with the Giants and Pittsburgh Steelers, became a Super Bowl hero when he caught the winning touchdown pass in the last minute of the Giants' 17-14 upset win over the previously unbeaten New England Patriots in Super Bowl XLII.

Burress was transported to Rikers Island jail in New York, where he arrived at 1:20 p.m. ET, according to Steve Morello, a deputy commissioner with the New York City Department of Corrections.

Burress was moved Wednesday morning to Ulster Correctional Facility, a medium-security prison, in Napanoch, N.Y., on the edge of Catskill State Park. There, he will undergo further processing, including getting state-issue clothing and a strip search.

**NOTE:** In Mississippi, this would probably have been a fine of up to $500, although it would have been up to the police officer's discretion. Most that I have known throughout my career would have considered the pain he suffered as enough punishment and probably would not have even charged him unless the establishment pushed the issue.

**BAD NEWS:**

This map came from: http://www.handgunlaw.us/states/mississippi.pdf

It is in color depicting states in either red or light blue. Since this book is printed in black and white, the red shows up as the darker states. They do not accept our conealed weapons permits as of now. So imagine you are driving to New Hampshire to visit relatives and want to carry your weapon with you. Do you face the same delimia that our young Marine and Pro Football player face? No, because we will choose not to carry it on our person. We may until we get to Virginia or West Virginia depending on the route we choose but after that we store it.

So you ask, "how does that work?" Well our US Congress was not totally stupid when they passed federal law that limited what states could impose upon us if we are only moving a weapon through their state and not carrying it under our jacket. Congress passed a federal law titled, "Interstate Transportation of Firearms" (United States Code, Title 18, Section 926A). Again though, I am not an attorney and do not give legal advice, so before you go, contact your attorney and ask him/her to review the law and advise you of how you should go about transporting and storing your firearm.

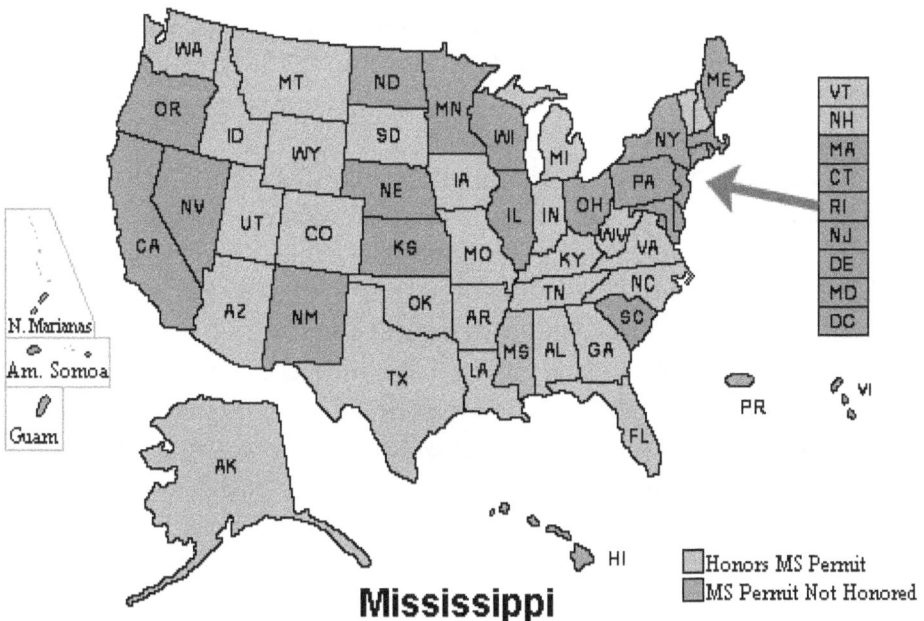

**Mississippi**

Honors MS Permit
MS Permit Not Honored

**THE GOOD NEWS:**

18 USC § 926A - Interstate transportation of firearms

*Notwithstanding any other provision of any law or any rule or regulation of a State or any political subdivision thereof, any person who is not otherwise prohibited by this chapter from transporting, shipping, or receiving a firearm shall be entitled to transport a firearm for any lawful purpose from any place where he may lawfully possess and carry such firearm to any other place where he may lawfully possess and carry such firearm if, during such transportation the firearm is unloaded, and neither the firearm nor any ammunition being transported is readily accessible or is directly accessible from the passenger compartment of such transporting vehicle: Provided, That in the case of a vehicle without a compartment separate from the driver's compartment the firearm or ammunition shall be contained in a locked container other than the glove compartment or console. (Source-Cornell Law Center)*

**TRANSPORTING ON AIRCRAFT:**

You say, well that all sounds good, but I don't have relatives in New Hampshire that I plan to visit. I have friends who are going to Nevada on a hunting trip and they have invited me to go. Although I use a rifle for hunting, I never go into the woods without my backup handgun on my side. I want to take it with me to Nevada and I'm not driving, rather flying commercial. What can I do?

Lucky you, the rules are pretty much the same with regards to transporting in that you cannot have a weapon in the passenger compartment with you. Other rules apply that require you to declare that you have the firearm in your possession. Rather than try and paraphrase the Transportation Security Administration (TSA) rules, I have copied them directly from their website and inserted on the succeeding pages for you. Again, as always though, just to be on the safe side, you might want to check with an attorney before proceeding. Boy, they ought to pay me big bucks after this book comes out. :-)

## TRAVELING ON AIRCRAFT WITH SPECIAL ITEMS:

### Firearms & Ammunition

Travelers may only transport UNLOADED firearms in a locked, hard-sided container in or as checked baggage. All firearms, ammunition and firearm parts, including firearm frames and receivers, are prohibited in carry-on baggage.

Firearm possession laws vary by state and locality. Travelers should familiarize themselves with state and local firearm laws for each point of travel prior to departure.

Airlines may have additional requirements for traveling with firearms and ammunition. Travelers should also contact the airline regarding firearm and ammunition carriage policies.

Also, please note that other countries have different laws that address transportation and possession of firearms. If international travel is planned traveling internationally, check the regulations of the destination country to ensure compliance with their requirements.

There are certain limited exceptions for law enforcement officers who may fly armed by meeting the requirements of Title 49 CFR § 1544.219. Law enforcement officers should read our policies on traveling with guns.

Failure to adhere to the following regulations will preclude passengers from traveling with firearms, ammunitions or firearm parts:

Travelers must declare all firearms to the airline during the ticket counter check-in process.

The firearm must be unloaded.

The firearm must be in a hard-sided container.

The container must be locked. A locked container is defined as one that completely secures the firearm from being accessed. Locked cases that can be pulled open with little effort cannot be brought aboard the aircraft.

If firearms are not properly declared or packaged, TSA will provide the bag to law enforcement for resolution with the airline. If the issue is resolved, law enforcement will release the bag to TSA so screening may be completed.

TSA must resolve all alarms of checked luggage. If a locked container containing a firearm alarms, TSA will contact the airline, who will make a reasonable attempt to contact the owner and advise the passenger to go to the screening location. If contact is not made, the container will not be placed on the aircraft.

If a locked container alarms during screening and is not marked as containing a declared firearm, TSA will cut the lock in order to resolve the alarm.

Travelers should remain in the area designated by the aircraft operator or TSA representative to take the key back after the container is cleared for transportation.

Travelers must securely pack any ammunition in fiber (such as cardboard), wood or metal boxes or other packaging specifically designed to carry small amounts of ammunition.

Firearm magazines and ammunition clips must be securely boxed or included within a hard-sided case containing an unloaded firearm.

Small arms ammunition, including ammunition not exceeding .75 caliber for a rifle or pistol and shotgun shells of any gauge, may be carried in the same hard-sided case as the firearm, as long as it follows the packing guidelines described above.

TSA prohibits black powder or percussion caps used with black-powder. These regulations are strictly enforced. Violations can result in state and local criminal prosecution, as well as civil penalties of up to $2,000 per charge.

I have to tell you a story very near and dear to my heart. It has to do with taking a firearm into an airport and it has to do with Mississippi Law as it pertains to shotguns as concealed weapons.

I lost my youngest daughter in a car wreck on September 11, 1998. A year and a half later, I went back into the military after a six year break. I arrived at Naval Weapons Station Earle, New Jersey right after the July 4th holiday. My new job as a Navy Lieutenant in the law enforcement, and physical security field was head of security for the entire northeast region of the United States. I oversaw all Navy security departments from New Jersey to Maine.

My wife who was still living in Mississippi, decided to fly up and be with me on the anniversary of our daughter's death so we could deal with the depression together. I had tried to keep myself busy and found that hunting on base for deer and geese was very good. I didn't have a goose gun and needed one with a long barrel to reach high where they flew over. I contacted my friend Ryan Hood in Jackson, a firearms dealer and had him order me a Browning 10 guage goose gun. I had my wife pick it up and bring it to me when she would leave on September 8, 2001. She planned to spend a few days with me and fly back home on September 11, 2001 so she could put flowers on our daughter's grave in Magee, Mississippi.

If you are paying much attention to these dates, you realize that we were all about to face a new era of taking guns into airports due to the attacks on our country the date she was scheduled to fly back home.

While sitting in my New Jersey office on September 8, 2001, I received a frantic phone call from my wife. She was being held by the Jackson Airport Police after placing my shotgun on the conveyor belt and every siren in the place went off. She said they were about to take her to book her in at the Rankin County Sheriff's Office. I blew a fuse.

She explained to me that she arrived slightly later than she would have liked, but the problem was worsened by two cancelled aircraft. The lobby area was packed with panicky passengers. She had a suitcase in one hand and a large gun case in the other. A flight attendant stood up on the scales over the crowd and told people if they were on the New York flight to go down the corridor and their baggage would be checked plane side. The attendant could not see my wife below her shoulders and my wife did what she was told. She expected somebody from the plane to take the bags around the conveyor to the tarmac and put them on the aircraft.

At that time, I don't think they checked every bag at the counter, although they did check everything that went through the conveyor. Again there was a huge crowd at the conveyor. When she got there, the security person told her to put the bags on the conveyor. She tried to explain that one of them was a gun without saying the word "gun." The hard black plastic case had an engraving of a man shooting a shotgun with a Labrador Retriever at his side. This case was very long and in the shape of a gun. There could be no question in anybody's mind that it was a gun case and likely contained a gun. The attendant, acting very frustrated insisted that she put it on the conveyor. She did and that's when all hell broke loose.

I contacted the airport police, some of whom I knew and asked them to allow her passage and I would straighten out this matter as soon as possible. They finally agreed but retained my new shotgun without allowing her to travel with it.

She arrived a litle late, but that was okay given the circumstances. Upon her arrival, I immediately started calling FBI friends and so forth. I learned very quickly, within a day or so that the FBI did not intend to prosecute her on a criminal charge given the extenuating circumstances. However, there was still the question that the FAA may impose a civil fine of up to $500 at the time. While I didn't like that as a possibility, I was prepared to pay the fine since there would be no criminal charges even though I don't think she did anything wrong.

On September 10th, I received a call from the FAA in Nashville, Tennessee indicating they would not be imposing a civil fine given the circumstances. My wife was still by my side in New Jersey preparing to fly home the next day.

There was only one other issue to resolve. That was to get the gun back from the Jackson Airport Police and make sure she would not be arrested upon her return (which she was sweating big time). I made a phone call to the Airport Police and talked to the "arresting" officer. He told me they intended to keep the gun and charge her. I blew another fuse over the phone. I demanded, "Charge her with what?" His response to me was that since the FBI and FAA were not interested, they would charge her with "Carrying a Concealed Weapon" under Mississippi Law. Sound familiar?

Little did this guy know, I knew Mississippi Weapons Laws inside and out and I had no intentions of taking this lying down. I asked to speak to the Chief and was given the runaround.

My wife had been seen off on that trip by a former co-worker of mine at the Attorney General's Office (now at the Rankin County Sheriff's Office. At the time of my wife's trip this lady was working in the Jackson Airport Police Department. I contacted her and asked if she could explain to them that we weren't criminals and I knew the law. I think she did all she could, but to no avail.

I knew from past cases of my own as a police officer in Mississippi that the legislature was very protective of hunter's rights and would not include shotguns or rifles in the defintion of concealed weapons in the statute unless they had been sawed off below the legal limit. However, just to be sure, I went online from New Jersey and researched Mississippi's law at the time. It had not changed in that regard.

I called the young "arresting" officer again and demanded that he read the law, Section 97-37-1 of the Misissippi Code, titled "Deadly weapons; carrying while concealed; use or attempt to use; penalties." He had a copy of the law, but didn't know, or understand what it said. Here it is. Pay close attention to the bold print.

*(1) Except as otherwise provided in Section 45-9-101, any person who carries, concealed in whole or in part, any bowie knife, dirk knife, butcher knife, switchblade knife, metallic knuckles, blackjack, slingshot, pistol, revolver, or **any rifle with a barrel of less than sixteen (16) inches in length, or any shotgun with a barrel of less than eighteen (18) inches in length**, machine gun or any fully automatic firearm or deadly weapon, or any muffler or silencer for any firearm, whether or not it is accompanied by a firearm, or uses or attempts to use against another person any imitation firearm, shall upon conviction be punished as follows:*

I said to him then that I could go out to my car, cut a slice all the way across the entire seat, stuff my shotgun down into it, cover the sliced seat with duct tape, sit on top of it and a shotgun (unless sawed off below 18 inches) <u>COULD NOT</u> in any shape, fashion or form, be considered a concealed weapon by our law. I insisted that he take that to his Chief and prosecutors with a copy of the incident report and a photograph of the shotgun.

I really thought common sense would prevail in this situation. First of all, what kind of idiot would try to pass off a shotgun through the metal detector, in a clearly marked shotgun case? Secondly, the shotgun was packed in cosmoline and wrapped in wax paper. It was totally disassembled and had never been fired. There was no ammunition either with the gun or carried separately. It had not one, not two but three locks on the case.

During my last contact with the Airport Police Department, I felt like they would understand they had screwed up. I was right. They did and not only did they release my shotgun upon her return, they failed to press any charges. Good move on their part. I'll bet they know the law now. However, my wife was not able to fly on September 11, 2001. Nobody could.

I drove her to LaGuardia Airport in New York that morning. We left the base in New Jersey at about 6:30 a.m. and got to the airport in only an hour and a half. It was a beautiful warf, sunny, morning. I stood at the ticket counter and watched he get on the plane. I waived good-bye as they closed the door to the entrance corridor of the aircraft a few minutes after 8 a.m. I walked downstairs, used the restroom and then walked immediately to my truck. As I got out on the Brooklyn-Queen's Expressway headed back to New Jersey with the Manhattan skyline clear, I noticed smoke coming from one of the Twin Towers. As an Antiterrorism and Force Protection Officer, I kept up with terrorist activities and was aware of the previous bombing of one of the towers.

I got on my cell phone and called my boss in New Jersey. He always watched CNN from his office. I told him what I saw and asked if there was anything on the news about it. He turned on CNN and told me they were saying a plane had just hit the tower. As I moved closer to Brooklyn, more news came out over the radio and my phone went dead. I was able to reach my boss once more and while we were talking, I saw the second plane hit the other tower. By then the streets were full of fire trucks, ambulances, police cars, police motorcycles, unmarked cars, state police, FBI and everybody and their brother.

While concerned about a terrorist attack and dealing with the now very heavy traffic, I was more concerned with whether or not my wife's plane was one of the ones that struck the tower. I could do nothing now, with no phone service but creep along in traffic. My truck was running hot and I had to roll the windows down. Just as I passed under the Brooklyn Bridge with Manahatten across the river to my right, the first tower collapsed.

Ash drifted all the way across the river and settled on my truck's dashboard before I rolled the windows back up. My hands were tied. I was in charge of all Navy Law Enforcement and Security in the entire northeast and I couldn't leave the interstate or communicate on my cell phone. My subordinates had to shift the bases into THREATCON DELTA while I made my way back to New Jersey over five hours later, even though it only took an hour and a half in the other direction a few hours earlier.

My wife and her fellow passengers had been taken off their plane at the last minute. They rushed to find taxi cabs and hotel rooms. Several families had to share single rooms that day. I finally got an e-mail from her about 7:35 that night from her hotel business office. She was able to make it back across to New Jersey the next morning on a ferry. She stayed with me several more days since no planes were flying. She eventually made it to Atlanta by bus and shared a rental car from there to Jackson with a Jackson nurse she had met on the bus.

She really didn't want to go back through the Jackson Airport anyway and still felt she may be arrested, especially given everything that had happened since then, knowing how security would be even tighter. She picked my shotgun up a few days later after I convinced her I had talked to the police and they weren't going to arrest her.

I didn't feel too badly about the police even though they didn't know their job or the law to the extent that I thought they should. I was a little taken back by the insistence on them wanting to make a charge no matter what, but I let it pass.

I didn't feel such arrogance or ignorance again until I recently attended a class and brought this issue up in the presence of a University of Mississippi Police Officer who insisted, he would arrest anybody anyway if they brought a weapon in his jurisdiction. The attitude of some people is that they will make you pay through your time and attorney fees even if they can't convict you. As a former police administrator, I would fire an officer with that attitude. There are too many good ones out there and this is the kind that make the good ones look bad.

I later looked at the crime reports online submitted by that department and I can see why they have the need to go out and look for crime, reporting mostly thefts, one assault and no other crime of violence. They have too much time on their hands.

That's my story and I'm sticking to it.

The text of the Second Amendment

is

"A well-regulated Militia, being
necessary to the security
of a free State, the right of the
people to keep and bear Arms,
shall not be infringed."

# CHAPTER NINE

## Buying and Selling Weapons

Before purchasing or selling a weapon, there are several things you need to know and consider. Dealer sales differ from sales by private individuals. You should also consider your needs and limitations, as well as your desires of functionality.

**Retail Sales:**

Retail stores like Bass Pro and Dick's Sporting Goods are chain stores that deal in guns in Mississippi. There are also a number of "mom and pop" stores that usually supplement their gun sales with pawn items and the like. If they sell guns, they must be licensed by the Bureau of Alcohol Tobacco and Firearms as gun dealers. Those dealers who sell guns to individuals and buyers who purchase guns from them are required to complete their respective sections of ATF Form 4473. The dealer is required to run an immediate check on the buyer to determine if there is anything that would disqualify that person from buying a gun.

**Gun Shows:**

People who sell guns at gun shows are dealers just as the dealers at retail outlets or pawn shops. They are responsible for the same background checks and paperwork before selling a gun to anybody. The real advantage of these shows is the huge selection of both new and used guns, as well as ammunition and associated gear. Trades are also common, but you cannot negate the paperwork, or qualifications. The downside compared to regular retail outlets is that you have to pay an entry fee just to go in and look, but it is usually only a few dollars. They are most often held at the Fairgrounds in Jackson and other areas usually well-advertised throughout the year. Local dealers also buy tables and sell their wares there as well.

**Internet Sales:**

The typical internet retail sites like Amazon, E-Bay, etc., do not sell guns. However, there are internet auction and retail sites where you as an individual can purchase guns. Any of the dot com sites like gunsamerica, thegunsource, gunbroker, and others sell guns online to private individuals. However, in order for you to receive that gun, it must be shipped to a dealer in your area and you must arrange for that dealer to receive it. Once the gun is received, the dealer will contact you. After that, you will go down and fill out the ATF form and pay the dealer whatever you negotiated for his efforts. Certain black powder and air guns are exempt from those requirements and may be shipped directly to you in Mississippi.

**Private Sales:**

Private individuals may sell guns to other private individuals in Mississippi without completing ATF forms or any other paperwork, although a bill of sale is not a bad idea. The problem with this type sale is the buyer could be a convicted felon and you have no way, or obligation to run a criminal background check on the buyer. If you are the seller, you risk selling a gun to a convicted felon who may go out and commit a crime with that weapon. You could face civil action and possibly criminal action if it is later determined that you knew the person was a felon. You might be considered an accessory to his crimes, but then again, that's something you need to discuss with a lawyer.

**Buyer Considerations:**

A buyer should think like a military specification purchasing agent when buying a gun, in my opinion. What does that mean? It means you tell the seller exactly what you are looking for. You make it known every bell and whistle you want and then let the seller give you a price. It may be what you are looking for, but it may be a little too much. You may have to make certain concessions with your purchase. I would list the priority demands first and the other less important bells and whistles below those.

For example:

Semi-Automatic

American Made

Under $500

.40-.45 Caliber

.22 Caliber Conversion Capable

Must fire without magazine inserted

Ambidextrous safety

De-Cocking lever

Night Sights

Minimum 12 round magazine

Polymer Construction

Plastic Grips

Barrel length 3 ½ to 5 inches

These requirements tell the dealer right up front that there is no need to show you a revolver. Your first and highest priority is a semi-automatic so that is the only type pistol he will need to consider. The fact that American made is a high priority for you will rule out many top name brand semi-automatics like Glock, Sig Sauer, Heckler and Koch, etc. It may even mean that one manufacturer, such as Smith and Wesson will be the only maker capable of meeting your needs. The rest of your wants will have to be considered from there.

The calibers are pretty standard and it won't be hard to get a .40 or .45 caliber produced by any of the manufacturers. However, when you start to consider what is and is not capable of being easily and quickly converted to a .22 caliber, you may find that the American manufacturer won't be able to accommodate you. At that point, if that is the case, you may have to make a concession and tell the dealer you will forgo the American made requirement to get your conversion capable weapon.

If I were a dealer (and I am not), I might recommend a weapon that meets most of your needs that is made in Italy but imported and sold by US personnel, so you are not displacing US jobs and still getting a quality weapon.

I raise this issue because many people buy weapons that they cannot afford to shoot. I have mentioned many times in this book that in order to be proficient, you must practice, practice and practice more. If you are like the average person, you have not budgeted for and may not be able to budget for a large ammunition cost. For instance, you may pay in upwards of seventy cents per round for .40 caliber ammunition. With fifty-round qualification courses, that won't take long to eat into your pocket. On the other hand, you could have bought .22 caliber rounds for about three cents per round. So you would spend $1.50 instead of $35.00. That is a big difference. You say, "yes, but I don't want a .22 caliber. I want a .40 caliber.

"That's fine," I would say because you can get a .40 caliber European American Armory (EAA) "Witness" Tanfaglio (Italian made) with a .22 caliber conversion kit that you can change out in a minute or so. You still shoot the same weapon with the same feel. The only difference is recoil. However, don't pay much attention to that. Most police officers involved in shootings have reported that they didn't even notice the recoil. You will notice the difference on the range. But if $35 to a $100 a day on the range will keep you from going and $1.50 to $5.00 would allow you to go, I highly recommend this option. You could practice over and over with the .22 and not leave the range before shooting one box of .40 caliber just so you can remember the recoil and shot recovery. For most of us, it is the only option that will allow us to practice.

I purchased an EAA Witness through an online auction last year for $300. It was an early model but brand new and an excellent buy. They typically sell between $380 and $500 with the conversion slide and magazine another $200. I have owned guns all my adult life and have never lost a dollar on a sale. Good guns retain their value and you may find that you can own a gun for five years and sell it for a profit. They are an excellent investment. However, I have never owned a handgun that I liked more than my EAA Witness, primarily because I can afford to shoot it and it has the looks, feel and most of the bells and whistles I desired. I only had to make a few concessions. You may not have to make any.

This is a good looking gun, good feeling gun, and well made gun. It is reasonably priced for a high quality weapon and not only can you convert it to a .22 caliber with a conversion kit like the one below, you can buy one frame that will accomodate any of their calibers. So you don't have to convert it to a .22. If you want, you can convert it to any of the other calibers and still only have one frame. I don't know of any other manufacturer that makes a weapon with that capability.

The only thing I don't like is that the magazines I have been able to find for the .22 caliber are plastic. I like to be able to hit the magazine ejector button and have the magazine fall out quickly from its own weight. I didn't find that possible with my plastic magazine. However, I sanded it down, modifying it myself until I was able to obtain the ejection that I liked. It only took a little work. There may be metal magazines for the .22 out there. I just haven't seen them. If I find one, I will buy it and suggest you look for one if you buy this weapon and conversion kit.

## Post-Purchase

Once you have bought your weapon, when you go home, record the serial number. You may also want to photograph the weapon from all angles and do a close-up on the serial number. If the weapon gets stolen, you need to be able to provide this information to the responding law enforcement agency immediately. They will enter it into the National Crime Information Center (NCIC) Computer. If a police officer stops a car any time after that point and finds the weapon in the suspect's car, he can run a check to see if the weapon is listed as stolen. Without that information, it cannot be entered.

When I was an investigator at the DeSoto County Sheriff's Department in the late 1970's, we were having a lot of burglars come down from Memphis only 20 miles away. Guns were the hottest items.

One day I responded to a call and a young man had just gotten home from work. He was sick over the fact that a burglar had gotten his gun collection. When I asked for the serial numbers, he didn't have any of them. We couldn't put them on NCIC and if an officer ran across the weapons, he would have no way of knowing they were stolen. I talked to the victim about a week later and he was somewhat happier. The insurance company paid him, but that didn't help with the war relic or childhood guns his grandfather had given him for his first hunt. He said he learned his lesson and had bought a safe for his new guns. He had copied down all the new serial numbers.

About six months later, I got a call to go back to his house. He was leaning against the trunk of his car in the driveway wiping tears from his eyes. I said, "don't tell me they got your guns again." He just stood there, hands over his eyes, shaking his head up and down while sniffling. I said, "well, I know you you wrote the serial numbers down, so let me go ahead and get those while I write up the report." He started sniffling louder and shaking his head back and forth, trying to utter the word, "no."

He had indeed copied down the serial numbers, but he put them in the safe with the guns and this time the thieves took the entire safe with the guns and serial numbers inside. The safe was a stand-up type locker and was pretty heavy, but it was not bolted to the wall or floor.

**Don't let this happen to you!**

Just a few of the FBI's National Crime Information Center (NCIC) files:

■ Gun File—Records on stolen, lost, and recovered weapons and weapons used in the commission of crimes that are designated to expel a projectile by air, carbon dioxide, or explosive action.

■ Vehicle File—Records on stolen vehicles, vehicles involved in the commission of crimes, or vehicles that may be seized based on federally issued court order.

■ License Plate File—Records on stolen license plates.

■Protection Order File—Records on individuals against whom protection orders have been issued.

■Supervised Release File—Records on individuals on probation, parole, or supervised release or released on their own recognizance or during pre-trial sentencing.

■ Wanted Persons File—Records on individuals (including juveniles who will be tried as adults) for whom a federal warrant or a felony or misdemeanor warrant is outstanding.

■ National Sex Offender Registry File—Records on individuals who are required to register in a jurisdiction's sex offender registry.

In 2009, an NCIC off-line search on a license plate number revealed the plate was linked to a vehicle owned by a man wanted for the July 2008 murder of his mother in Mississippi. About an hour after receiving the search request, NCIC staff provided the results to the requesting agency, and that agency contacted a sheriff's office in Florida that had queried the plate two weeks earlier. Around 5 a.m. on April 18, three deputies from the Florida sheriff's office located the vehicle while responding to another call. When the deputies approached the vehicle, the suspect pulled a sawed-off shotgun from under a blanket and pointed the weapon at the deputies. The deputies shot and killed the suspect before he could fire.

# CHAPTER TEN

## Post-Shooting Considerations

Assume the worst case scenario has arrived. You as a concealed weapon permit holder have had to shoot someone. The person is lying there, but you are not a doctor and don't know if they are dead or not. You don't know if they are playing dead waiting on you to make yourself vulnerable so they can surprise you with a bullet. You may feel a legal obligation to render first aid.

I can't tell you what to do with regards to rendering first aid but I will tell you it is dangerous to approach someone who has tried to kill you and you aren't sure if they are dead or not. Remember the pharmacist case in Oklahoma I mentioned? To go over and finish the suspect off with additional rounds in their body while they are incapacitated is clearly not the right thing to do. The police, grand jury, prosecutor, jury and trial judge were all convinced what started out as a justifiable self-defense in that case, escalated to murder.

Everything depends on the circumstances that could differ so widely. But first and foremost, it would probably be wise to continue to hold your gun on the suspect and call with one hand or better yet have someone else call 911. The "victim" in this case, as he will be called may have friends, family or supporters nearby and the situation could get ugly real fast, especially if it occurred in a public place.

Best case scenario would be to hold your weapon on the person until the police get there. But this gets tricky. Police officers often don't get enough information when they are dispatched, to make a good assessment of the scene. They may only know that one guy shot another one at this location. If you are standing there with gun in hand when the police walk up, you could very well get shot yourself. Somebody needs to greet the police officer unarmed. The gun should be out of the way, not seen by the police until he asks for it.

For crime scene investigative purposes, it should not be handled by anyone else, but should not be in a location so as to put the officer in fear of his life. Hopefully, when someone called 911, they dispatched not only the police, but an ambulance and the appropriate medical personnel can assume responsibility for the injured (or deceased) person. Some states, like Michigan have laws requiring the "shoot-er" to render aid to the "shoot-ee".

**Michigan Statute 752.842 Firearms; discharging; injuries. Sec. 2.**

*Any person who discharges a firearm and thereby injures or fatally wounds another person, or has reason to believe he has injured or fatally wounded another person, shall immediately stop at the scene and shall give his name and address to the injured person, or any member of his party, and shall render to the person so injured immediate assistance and reasonable assistance in securing medical and hospital care and transportation for such injured person.*

Since Michigan honors our resident permits, you may want to know this tidbit of information if you plan to travel there. At least it is something to think about and could become a requirement here in time. Many people will bring up the Mississippi Good Samaritan Law which is designed to prevent civil action against someone acting in good faith in rendering emergency medical care.

**§73-25-37. Liability of physicians, dentist, nurses or emergency medical technician for rendering emergency care.**

*No duly licensed, practicing physician, dentist, registered nurse, licensed practical nurse, certified registered emergency medical technician, or any other person who, in good faith and in the exercise of reasonable care, renders emergency care to any injured person at the scene of an emergency, or in transporting said injured person to a point where medical assistance can be reasonably expected, shall be liable for any civil damages to said injured person as a result of any acts committed in good faith and in the exercise of reasonable care or omissions in good faith and in the exercise of reasonable care by such persons in rendering the emergency care to said injured person.*

How old is the concept of the Good Samaritan Law?

*The concept of the Good Samaritan is from the biblical story of the benevolent acts, along the road from Jerusalem to Jericho, by a Good Samaritan who helped a man who had been attacked by a gang of robbers. What may be forgotten is that there were others who passed by the man without stopping. A priest, "when he saw the man...went by on the other side of the road." In the same way, a temple official came along. When he saw the man, he also went by on the other side. However, it was the "foreigner from Samaria" who was "filled with compassion and went to help." Luke 10:25-37*

However, this is another area where you need to talk to your lawyer. I doubt seriously that you as a private citizen (unlike public servants) have a legal duty or obligation to render first aid to somebody that you were forced to shoot in order to save your own life. But, if you do so on your own free will, the Good Samaritan Law <u>may</u> protect you.

## CRIME SCENE:

I am going to tell you what the police will want you to do regarding the shooting. In doing so, I am assuming that you were within your rights and did exactly what you were supposed to do. Your lawyer may not want you to extend your hand of cooperation this far, especially if he thinks there might be some question as to your innocence. It is very hard for me to take off my police hat. I can tell you if you deviate from some of the items though, you may be deemed to have tampered with the crime scene and may face charges of obstructing justice, so you have to balance how much you want to listen to your lawyer at this point with how much you want to please the police.

Ideally the lawyers' desires and the policemens' desires should coincide, but that's not always the case. Bottom line is though, you don't want to piss of the police and appear suspicious after you have executed a perfectly legal shooting. The decision as to whether or not to arrest you after the shooting weighs heavily on him. He may feel confident that you did what you had to do and have continued to cooperate with no reason for him to make an arrest. That may be overturned by the prosecutor later and he may bring the case before the grand jury either to investigate, or to seek an indictment against you. If that happens, you will not likely be called to participate.

**POST-SHOOTING STEPS:**

Protect yourself.

Wait on the police and do not disturb the scene.

Render the firearm safe if possible.

Ask all witnesses to remain, but not discuss the circumstances among themselves until the police have had time to interview each of them separately.

Do not allow people to walk around the scene.

Do not attempt to clean up any blood, or other bodily fluids that may be present at that time.

Do not wash or wipe your hands until the police tell you it is okay.

Do not pick up any spent casings.

Do not disturb any video if it is running, but notify the police if you are aware of it.

If you want to have your lawyer present before you make a statement to the police, you have that right. However, you may end up in jail first waiting to track your lawyer down.

Commence cleanup ONLY after the police have authorized it.

Don't speak to the media until you have discussed it with your lawyer and consider having your lawyer present during any interviews.

# ABOUT THE AUTHOR

Rick Ward was born in Tunica, Mississippi, on August 1, 1953. He enlisted in the US Navy during the Vietnam era and was honorably discharged in 1975. He remained in the navy reserves for over thirty years. He has an Associate degree in law enforcement from Mississippi Gulf Coast Community College, a B.S. in criminal justice from the University of the State of New York, and a Master's in education from the University of Hawaii. He is a graduate of the Mississippi State Police Academy, the U.S. Army Military Police School, and the FBI National Academy. He is a Certified Protection Professional (CPP) by the American Society of Industrial Security and certified level five of five in Homeland Security.

Rick retired in 2005 with a dual career in civilian, and US Navy law enforcement. His career netted him a total of thirty-four years combined military and civilian law enforcement experience as he traveled the world.

Twice during Rick's naval career, he was stationed at the shipyard in Pascgaoula. During that time he was instrumental in teaching courses associated with firearms at three Mississippi police academies. His navy certfication and training as a Small Arms Military Instructor (SAMI) served him well when certified as an instructor by the Mississippi Board on Law Enforcement Standards and Training. During the early 1990's, he conducted judgmental shooting training at police and sheriff departments all over Mississippi, using a state of the art electronic firearms simulator. He provided executive protection and advanced firearms training in Pascagoula and the police academies at Pearl and Gulf Park.

Throughout his career, he has been a city patrol officer, undercover state narcotics officer, county criminal investigator, State Attorney General political corruption investigator, Gaming Commission division director and Federal Employment Compensation Act fraud investigator.

Between those various positions in civilian law enforcement, Rick served on active duty as investigator aboard a battleship, officer in charge of security for two major shore installations and an amphibious assault ship. He was a force protection officer for counter-drug operations in Central America and Regional Security Officer for the entire northeast coast.

Rick was on site in New York on September 11, 2001 and responsible for navy security reactionary forces. His last assignment with the Naval Criminal Investigative Service (NCIS) led to his position at headquarters in Washington, DC before retiring as a lieutenant commander on February 1, 2006.

He has written articles in military and civilian law enforcement journals with worldwide circulation throughout his career. In the last five years, he has written two legal suspense novels, one historical novel and one nonfiction expose' on state government.

Rick is a member of the "not so prestigious club" of having been shot in the line of duty.

# AUTHOR COMMENTS

There was a time early in my law enforcement career during the mid '70's that I thought only law enforcement personnel should carry guns. That all changed one day in 1976 when our Moss Point dispatcher sent me on a dusk-dark call, armed only with the information that a disturbance was in progress at a certain address. There was no mention of weapons involved.

When I arrived on scene, I was looking carefully to find the street address in a very low-class, unkept part of town. While looking to my left, I saw a flash of light out the corner of my eye. When I looked up, I saw the plastic wadding of a shotgun shell fall onto my windshield wiper blade. Immediately thereafter, I saw a pistol blast out the corner of my right eye.

It didn't take me long to realize that two idiots who lived across the street from each other were involved in a feudal shootout, and I was in their crossfire. I didn't know at the time if they had a beef with me being there, or if they were only trying to kill each other. I didn't want to stick around to find out.

I floorboarded the car and leaned over to the right, almost lying down on the seat, as I sped to the end of the short dead-end street. I spun the car around to use it for a shield, by then about three doors down, and still not knowing if I was a target, or just a hindrance to their efforts. I got outside my car and placed the shotgun over the hood and pulled the microphone out while calling for backup. There was no backup available.

Several "Rednecks" were working on a hotrod in the driveway adjacent to me. Beer cans cluttered the fenders. One who seemed very alert called out to me and said, "you need some help officer?" I said, "have y'all got guns?" One said, "Oh, yes sir, we got some here in the truck and more in the house. Want us to get 'em?" I had real second thoughts about these guys and had no idea how much beer they had consumed, but I needed help.

As it turned out, I handled the situation myself, but I realized after that, if anybody was friendly to me when I was about to be in a potential shootout, I wanted them on my side, and I certainly wanted them armed.

I changed my mind that day and began to believe that every person willing to defend himself, or help his fellow man in a fire fight, should be armed in accordance with the law if he had the desire to be.

Sadly, too many police officers feel their hands are tied when it comes to shooting. They are given so many intermediate tools like batons, cuffs, spray, and tasers. They are expected to use them first, only escalating to a firearm when all else has failed. They are constantly threatened with criminal charges, loss of jobs and civil suits, to the point that many are afraid to shoot. I personally think that has led to the death of many good officers.

Gary Kleck, Professor of Criminal Justice at Florida State University, in his carefully researched book *Point Blank: Guns and Violence in America,* found that "robbery and assault victims who used a gun to resist were less likely to be attacked or to suffer an injury than those who used any other methods of self-protection or those who did not resist at all."

Convicted felons revealed in his surveys that they were more afraid of armed citizens than they were of the police. And well they should be. "Armed citizens kill 2,000 to 3,000 criminals each year, three times the number killed by the police. And only two percent of civilian shootings involve an innocent person mistakenly identified as a criminal, whereas the error rate for the police is more than five times that high."

Stories mentioned herein about the beer-thief shot by the store clerk, burglars next door shot by the Texas resident, and the young lady from Oklahoma shooting the stalker as he broke through her door, are all signs of changing times. America is tired of criminal activity...dead tired of it. We are arming ourselves. More and more, lawmakers, prosecutors and jurors have our backs. Judges are establishing new case law that seems to continually favor the victim of a crime when he is forced to use deadly force. They are sending a message to would-be criminals. It is no longer a message of "do the crime and be preapred to do the time," rather a message of "do the crime and be prepared to meet thy maker."

Be responsible in the use of a firearm. Be even more responsible in using good judgment as to when you need to take someone's life, but don't be so intimidated by potential legal proceedings that it may cause you to lose your life for not acting. You have the inherent right to protect yourself. Use it, or lose it.

# DEDICATION

*I am dedicating this book to my son Brian, who at only thirty-eight years old has suffered about as many setbacks as I have at fifty-eight, but he has remained resilient.*

*Brian spent many hours with aches and pains as a teenager who "volunteered" to be my training dummy while at the same time, becoming certified, in the use of a PR-24 police side-handle baton.*

*He is an expert marksman and a strong believer in the second amendment to the constitution, and the right to bear arms. Brian has conducted relentless research and educated himself on firearms, ballistics, tactics, and their capabilities about as well as anybody I have ever known.*

*He served in the US Army in the early 1990's and was selected directly out of Airborne School, for the exclusive and prestigious "Old Guard" in Washington, DC. He participated in Army General Colin Powell's retirement, First Lady Jacqueline Kennedy Onassis' funeral and others, as well as laying to rest, many of our nation's heroes. The "Old Guard," made up of only the fittest, hand-picked, tall and lean soldiers was made famous by the Hollywood motion picture, "Gardens of Stone," starring James Caan, which glorified the thousands of soldiers they paid homage to daily, at Arlington and other national cemeteries. The elite soldiers, with their picture-perfect, poster image, were the first that foreign dignitaries would see on their celebrated visits to our country. I am honored that he was a part of it.*

*Brian plans to take part in concealed weapon training by converting a portion of his land near Jackson into a shooting range, while serving as a range coach and safety observer.*

*He has been instrumental in proofreading and offering sanity checks and recommendations for this book.*

*He is a great husband and father to three of my grandchildren.*

*I am very proud of him.*

*Rick Ward*

www.ingramcontent.com/pod-product-compliance
Lightning Source LLC
Chambersburg PA
CBHW030018290326
41934CB00005B/387